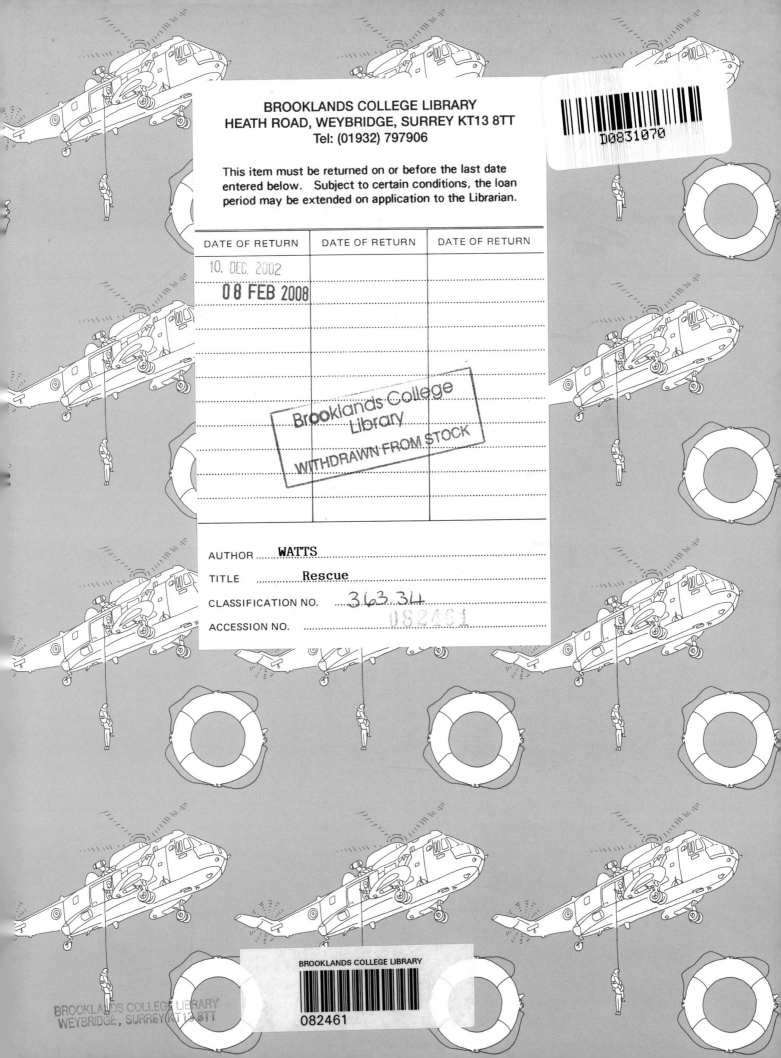

RESCUE

Special
Air Service
(SAS) badge

Rescue
helicopter

Military gas mask

US firefighter

Dutch ambulance

Mine-detector robot

Rigid
inflatable
lifeboat

Compass

DK EYEWITNESS GUIDES

French police force badge

RESCUE

Written by
CLAIRE WATTS

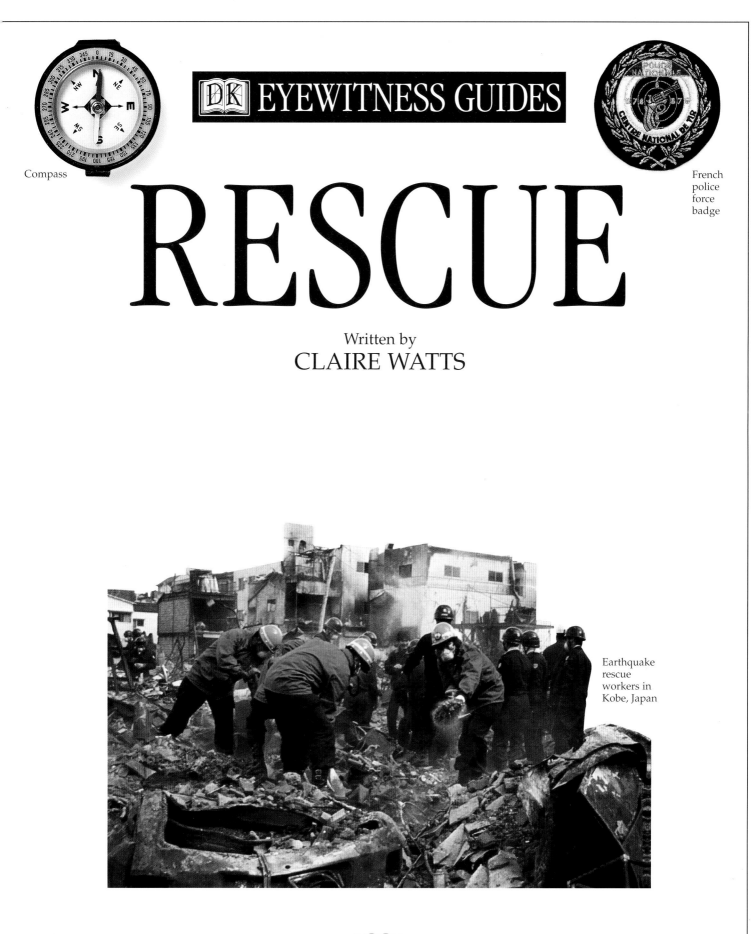

Earthquake rescue workers in Kobe, Japan

A Dorling Kindersley Book

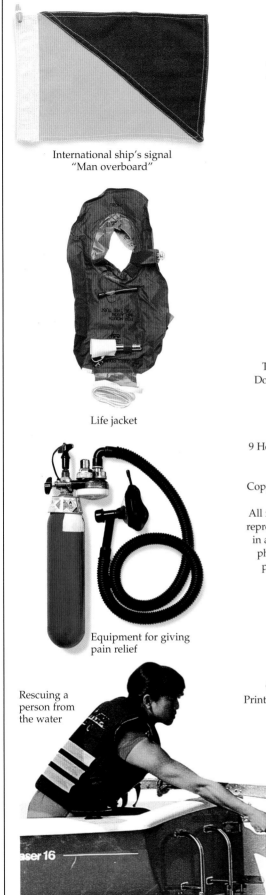

International ship's signal
"Man overboard"

Life jacket

Equipment for giving
pain relief

Rescuing a
person from
the water

Dorling DK Kindersley

LONDON, NEW YORK, SYDNEY, DELHI, PARIS,
MUNICH and JOHANNESBURG

Project editor Amanda Rayner
Art editor Ann Cannings
Senior editor Monica Byles
Senior art editor Jane Tetzlaff
Category publisher Jayne Parsons
Senior managing art editor Julia Harris
Production Kate Oliver
Picture research Mollie Gillard
Jacket designer Dean Price
DTP designers Almudena Díaz
and Matthew Ibbotson

This Eyewitness ® Guide has been conceived by
Dorling Kindersley Limited and Editions Gallimard

First published in Great Britain in 2001 by
Dorling Kindersley Limited
9 Henrietta Street, Covent Garden, London WC2E 8PS

A CIP catalogue record for this book is
available from the British Library.

ISBN 0 7513 1364 5

Colour reproduction by Colourscan, Singapore
Printed in China by Toppan Printing Co. (Shenzhen) Ltd

See our complete
catalogue at

www.dk.com

Mountaineers'
nylon rope

Stainless-steel
ladder

St Bernard dog

French fire engine

Contents

Firefighter in action

First on the scene

FIRST AIDERS
Basic medical treatment, such as dressing a patient's wounds or helping a person to breathe, is known as first aid. At sporting occasions and other busy public events, volunteer first aiders, including the St John Ambulance, are on hand to help if anyone is taken ill.

A SAILOR CLINGING TO THE HULL of an upturned boat, a starving child in a country stricken by famine, or an injured person trapped beneath rubble after an earthquake are all in terrible danger. All they can do is wait for their first glimpse or sound of emergency workers and hope that aid comes in time to save them. In any rescue operation, the priorities for the first rescue workers to arrive on the scene are to locate the people who need help and to assist those who are injured, trapped, or in danger, and take them to a place of safety. Only then can the rescue crew start to bring the emergency situation under control so that no other lives will be put at risk.

All-weather lifeboat

ON STANDBY
For many emergency crews, rescue work is only part of their life. They spend most of the time doing other jobs but are on standby in case a rescue situation occurs. When they receive an emergency call, they leave their work and rush to join the rest of the crew to operate lifeboats, take part in search and rescue missions, or fly off to an international disaster.

Airport fire truck

Flashing light

ROAD ACCIDENTS
An ambulance races to the scene of an accident, where paramedics treat the casualty, then contact the hospital to tell them what injuries the patient has suffered. This gives the hospital time to prepare any treatment needed before the patient arrives. In such incidents, the emergency services often work together. For example, the police may cordon off the area where the accident took place to prevent further casualties.

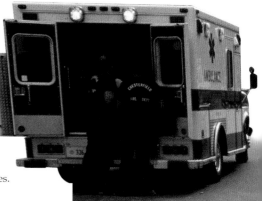

LIGHTS AND SIRENS
In any emergency, speed is critical to save lives and bring the situation under control. To hasten their journey to the scene, emergency vehicles have sirens and flashing lights to warn other traffic to get out of the way and distinctive colouring that makes them instantly recognizable.

EMERGENCY CALLS
The first thing to do in an emergency is to find a telephone and call the special emergency number (999 in the UK). Calls are directed to a central control room where an operator helps to decide which service is required. Details are then passed on to the appropriate rescue service, which immediately dispatches a rescue team to the scene.

Answering calls in the emergency control room

Red Cross
volunteer,
Ethiopia

Australian
paramedic

Medical equipment
is carried on the
motorbike

VOLUNTEERS
In addition to the professional
services, many rescue
workers are volunteers who
devote their spare time to
working in extremely difficult
circumstances to help those in
need. Like the professionals,
these volunteers also spend
time training to deal with
emergency situations.
Without volunteers, many
organizations would be
unable to deliver critical
humanitarian aid to victims
of accidents, natural disasters,
and other emergencies.

ARRIVING AT THE SCENE
When accidents happen in places that
are difficult to reach by road, rescue
services use versatile vehicles such
as motorbikes or helicopters. These
methods of transport are vital in cities,
where they can avoid traffic that
would delay other road vehicles.

Rescue worker
wheels casualty
to waiting
ambulance

Victim of a
car accident

Rescue stories

Robinson Crusoe

THE CRISIS AND DRAMA of a rescue situation make gripping stories, television programmes, and films. Ancient legends and fairy tales feature rescues from supernatural creatures such as monsters, demons, wicked witches, and giants. As the situation becomes desperate, a brave hero may rush in to save the day, helped by magical powers, great strength and cunning, or simple courage. Rescue stories involving life-threatening crises, heroism, and survival are as popular today as ever. Dramatic television series and disaster movies set in the world of the fire service, a hospital emergency department, or on board a lifeboat draw huge audiences, while documentary programmes following the emergency services in real-life situations turn rescue crews into popular heroes.

Superman
flies to the rescue

THE LITTLE MERMAID
Although most old tales tell of men or boys rescuing women or girls, in some stories a girl takes the lead. In *The Little Mermaid* by Hans Christian Andersen (1805–75), a mermaid rescues a prince from a shipwreck, then falls in love with him. The rescue of endangered sailors by beautiful and mysterious mermaids was a common theme in many folk and fairy tales.

CASTAWAY
Survival and rescue from a shipwreck make fascinating material for an adventure story. The best-known fictional castaway is Robinson Crusoe. The author, Daniel Defoe (1660–1731), based the story on real-life castaway Alexander Selkirk who quarrelled with his ship's captain and was left on an uninhabited island from 1704 until his rescue five years later.

MAN'S BEST FRIEND
Some of the greatest screen heroes are animals. The most famous is Lassie, the collie dog, who has starred in films since 1943. Based on the book *Lassie Come Home* by Eric Knight (1897–1943), Lassie's amazing adventures have included rescuing people from fires or drowning.

HERO TO THE RESCUE

Extraordinary powers, including X-ray vision, supersensitive hearing, incredible strength, and the ability to fly, give characters such as Superman the capacity to save the world. Some heroes, like James Bond, are specially trained and equipped with amazing gadgets, while others, such as Zorro, are armed only with bravery, cunning, and a sharp sword.

A scene from *The Towering Inferno*

NAIL-BITING DRAMA

One of greatest disaster movies ever made was *The Towering Inferno* (1974), the drama of a fire in a 135-storey building in San Francisco, USA. As in many of today's disaster movies, the central character is a maverick rescue worker who breaks the rules or risks his own life to rescue other people.

GEORGE AND THE DRAGON

Ancient legends, fairy tales, and even modern action movies feature heroic men who rescue women in danger and fight off their aggressors. The legend of St George is just such a tale. A princess is offered to a dragon as a human sacrifice, but St George arrives just in time to slay the beast and save the life of the princess.

St George battles with the dragon

9

Historical rescues

IN THE PAST, when an emergency occurred, the success of a rescue operation was usually a matter of chance. There were no easy ways of raising the alarm and few emergency services to call. With luck, someone nearby might be prepared to help an injured or trapped person, or run to fetch a doctor or fire engine. People lit beacon fires to attract help to an isolated spot or fired a shot to alert rescuers by boat. Little could be done to predict natural disasters such as volcanic eruptions and earthquakes, so people made offerings to the gods or carried lucky charms to try to prevent such disasters. Emergency medical treatment simply involved bandaging people as well as possible and amputating limbs that were too badly damaged to heal properly.

Body cast of a volcano victim from Pompeii

POMPEII
In AD 79, when the volcano Vesuvius erupted near Pompeii in Italy, the townspeople had no advance warning. Most of those who died were suffocated by the fumes. People in nearby Stabiae saw and heard the volcano before clouds of ash began to bury their town. They rushed away, many with cushions tied to their heads to protect themselves from the hail of debris.

Horse-drawn lifeboat

SHIPWRECK HEROINE
In 1838, a steamboat called the *Forfarshire* began to sink when it struck rocks on the northeast coast of England in a storm. Aged 23, Grace Darling (1815–42) and her father, the local lighthouse keeper, spotted the shipwreck and rowed out to sea, risking their lives to rescue survivors from the stricken ship.

SAN FRANCISCO EARTHQUAKE

When a huge earthquake hit San Francisco, USA, in 1906, the city was devastated. Fire swept through the streets for three days and two nights. Troops were brought in to stop the spread of the blaze by blowing up houses in the path of the fire, but ordinary people could do little other than watch the city burn. This photograph shows the terrible damage to Sacramento Street.

17th-century firefighting equipment

POUR ON WATER

Most cities are built near the coast or a river. In the past, this provided a vital source of water for putting out fires. Volunteers formed a human chain, passing full buckets from the river from hand to hand to the scene of the blaze. People used hand-held pumps to fight small fires and hooks to pull down buildings in the fire's path to stop it from spreading further.

LIFEBOATS

Until the end of the 18th century, most ships did not have lifeboats on board and relied on fishermen to rescue sailors in distress. Later, teams of horses dragged the first land-based lifeboats down the beach into the sea.

RUSHING TO THE SCENE

Early fire engines were usually owned by insurance companies. They raced to the scene of a fire but only tackled the blaze if their company's insurance badge was displayed on the burning building. The first fire engines were pumped by hand and had to be refilled with buckets. Steam-powered fire engines came into use in the USA in the mid-1800s.

Horse-drawn steam pumper fire engine, 1901

Technology to the rescue

RESCUE TODAY is a not a matter of chance as it was in the past, thanks to advances in technology, which have made extraordinarily difficult rescues possible. Communications equipment, from ordinary telephones to mobile phones and radio, alert emergency services to particular incidents. Searching devices locate lost or trapped people, and sophisticated equipment is used to contain problems such as fires, bombs, or chemical leaks, keeping damage to a minimum. Specially designed vehicles rush people to hospital, keeping them alive on the way, while advances in medicine mean that casualties who would previously have died from their injuries can now be saved. Even natural disasters such as hurricanes, earthquakes, and volcanic eruptions can often be predicted accurately enough to evacuate people to safety in time.

UPWARDLY MOBILE
The Hobo robot's six sturdy wheels and low centre of gravity allow it to climb steps easily, balancing at steep angles.

Water cannon fires a blast of water into the bomb to disable it

"MAYDAY!"
The invention of the wireless telegraph at the beginning of the 20th century enabled ships at sea to communicate with rescue services on land and with other vessels at sea. In an emergency, ships and planes usually broadcast a distress signal starting with the word "Mayday", which comes from the French phrase *m'aidez*, meaning "help me".

SEARCHING THE DEBRIS
To detect survivors trapped under a collapsed building after an earthquake or accident, rescue workers use a thermal-imaging camera, which clearly shows heat from the body of a living person amongst the cooler debris.

Firefighter using a thermal-imaging camera

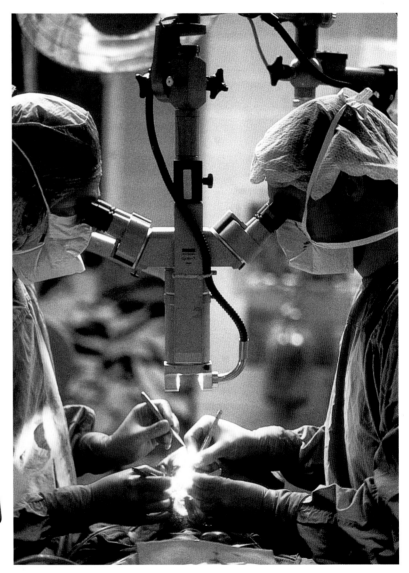

MICROSURGERY
One of the wonders of modern medicine is the ability to re-attach severed limbs. Every nerve, vein, and capillary must be joined for the limb to work properly. Surgeons use delicate instruments and watch their work through a binocular microscope, which gives an impression of three-dimensional depth. It can take as long as 19 hours to sew a hand back into place, with several surgeons working at the same time or in shifts.

Artificial satellites orbit the Earth, some from a height of 35,800 km (22,300 miles). They observe the planet and send back information to ground stations via microwaves or radio waves. Different satellites can be used to predict storms, monitor the movements of forest fires, detect changes in the shape of volcanoes, and even enable ships to keep track of their exact position at sea.

Arm camera

Shotgun used to gain access, for example, by shooting through a door lock

A telecommunications satellite in orbit

Rear video camera moves to scan the scene

BOMB DISPOSAL ROBOTS
Defusing unexploded bombs used to be an extremely dangerous job, which had to be done by hand. But in 1972, the first remote-controlled bomb disposal robot was invented. These robots can be steered towards a bomb or landmine and diffuse it while the human operator remains at a safe distance, watching a monitor linked to the robot's on-board cameras. This robot, called Hobo, has a mechanical arm and a water cannon to flush out explosives.

Member of ship's crew monitoring radar screens

Arm is moved up and down by the hydraulic cylinder

Radio control unit transmits to and from the operator

RADAR
Invented just before the start of World War II, radar sends out radio signals that reflect back off objects up to 3,200 km (2,000 miles) away to determine their position, size, and speed. Radar is used by ships, aircraft, and air-traffic control systems to avoid crashes and also to locate lost vessels and aircraft.

Hobo tele-operated bomb disposal robot

Drive camera is fixed in one position

Electrically driven wheels give Hobo a top speed of 4.8 km/h (3 mph)

13

The fire service

FIRE SPREADS THROUGH A BUILDING with terrifying speed, engulfing it in smoke and flames in minutes, cutting off the escape routes for people inside, and destroying the structure around them. Racing to the scene with its lights flashing and siren wailing, a fire engine is an unmistakable sight. Modern fire engines carry not only pumps and hoses to direct jets of water at the blaze, but every imaginable type of rescue equipment, from ropes and cutting tools to mops for cleaning up the mess. There are even special vehicles with no pumps or hoses at all, just ladders and cutting equipment. Many fire engines carry a special substance that can be added to the water as it pumps through the hoses to create foam. This foam can smother a fire so intense that water simply evaporates in the heat.

Axe

SPACE FOR STORAGE
Each fire engine has many lockers for storing essential rescue equipment. This locker (right) contains maps, tools, stretchers, backboards, breathing equipment, axes, street maps, and even plans of the area's sewerage system.

Inside a locker

Street maps

KEEPING IN TOUCH
The crew uses a two-way radio in the cab of the fire engine. This allows them to talk to operators in the control room and check on the situation at the scene of the fire.

Stretchers

A BIRD'S-EYE VIEW
Many fire engines have a protective cage on a hydraulic boom, which may be raised and turned, so that firefighters can be lifted high into the air. From this position, they bombard the flames from above using a hose that runs from the cage.

FIRE AXE
Firefighters have been using axes since the earliest days of the fire service. They are useful for tasks such as breaking down wooden doors in burning buildings.

Hydraulic boom

ABERDEEN

Serving Since 1889

102 FT.

TRUCK 231

EMERGENCY 911

HARFORD COUNTY

ABERDEEN 231 FIRE DEPT.

Outriggers provide stability

Locker

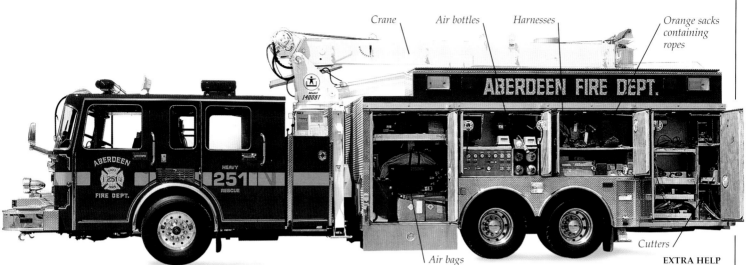

Crane   Air bottles   Harnesses   Orange sacks containing ropes

ABERDEEN FIRE DEPT.

Air bags

Cutters

EXTRA HELP
For some situations, a fire engine alone is not enough. This heavy rescue truck has a huge crane that extends 15 m (45 ft) to lift an overturned vehicle, or winch equipment to where it is needed. The truck also carries special panels and beams to stabilize walls in danger of collapse.

MANAGING THE EQUIPMENT
Firefighters have to know how to use each piece of equipment in the fire engine, from sharp cutters to high-pressure hoses (left). It is vital to check the equipment regularly to make sure that it is in working order and that it is stored in the correct place so it can be located quickly. Lost or broken equipment at the scene of a fire or an accident could cost lives.

DOWN TO SAFETY
To reach the tops of burning buildings, firefighters use extending ladders with a protective cage at the end. Such ladders are vital for bringing trapped people to safety. The crew locates survivors and helps each frightened person into the cage before bringing them carefully down to the ground. Some cages are equipped with nozzles at the front to spray a fine jet of water at the flames so that nobody inside is overcome by the heat.

Fighting the mighty blaze at Windsor Castle, UK, in 1992

Firefighters in action

SEARING FLAMES are not the only hazard that firefighters encounter. They also have to fight through blinding, choking smoke to rescue trapped people. High temperatures can make it difficult to breathe, and fire can weaken buildings so that walls and floors are in danger of collapse. Tackling blazes is only part of the job. Firefighters also deal with road accidents, train crashes, and even chemical leaks. To cope with such situations, all firefighters complete rigorous training, often in mock accidents that may be just as daunting as the real thing.

DOWN THE POLE
When the alarm sounds in the firestation, the firefighters immediately slide down a pole to reach their uniforms and fire engine. The pole is a much speedier way to get down than stairs, and a thick pad at the bottom cushions their landing.

Slippery metal pole

1 GETTING DRESSED
Uniforms are stored ready with the boots tucked into the trousers. Firefighters can step into both at once to save time.

Boots already inside trousers

2 PROTECTIVE TROUSERS
The firefighter's thick trousers are made of fireproof material and have braces to hold them up.

MONT BLANC TUNNEL DISASTER
A fire in a tunnel can be terrifying. Smoke quickly fills the tunnel so rescuers find it difficult to pinpoint the blaze and locate casualties. In 1999, a truck caught fire in the 11-km (7-mile) long Mont Blanc tunnel connecting France and Italy under the Alps. The fire burned for two days, but it took French, Swiss, and Italian firefighters almost a week to recover injured and dead people and clear away burnt-out vehicles.

Protective gloves

Breathing mask to protect against smoke

4 BREATHING APPARATUS
Once the air tank is on, the firefighter is ready to go. Firefighters can be dressed and in the fire engine in just 30 seconds.

3 JACKET ON
The jacket has luminous stripes so that the firefighter can be seen in thick smoke.

POUR ON WATER
Once the firefighters have connected the fire engine to the nearest mains water supply, the pumps start to feed the hoses. It takes several firefighters to control each hose when the powerful jet of water shoots towards the flames. In places where there is no piped water available, fire engines must carry their own supply.

The pressurized water jet is strong enough to knock a person down

SLICING THROUGH METAL
When people are caught in
a fire, a firefighter puts on
breathing apparatus and
plunges into the smoke to
rescue them before they are
overcome by the heat and
flames. Time is vital, so the
firefighter uses an electric
saw to slice through metal
doors or girders.

CAR CRASH
When a vehicle crashes, even if it does not immediately
catch fire, fuel lines may be damaged and leaking fuel
could ignite at any moment. The firefighters' first priority
is to rescue the driver and passengers. Often this can mean
cutting away the damaged vehicle around them using a
tool called the Jaws of Life. Foam is mixed with water and
sprayed around the vehicle to smother any leaking fuel.

*Heavy-duty
flame-retardant
gloves*

*Hard plastic
helmet with
wide brim
protects the neck
against sparks*

*The powerful electric
saw runs on batteries*

Trapped

Sᴛᴜᴄᴋ ɪɴsɪᴅᴇ ᴀ ᴄᴏʟʟᴀᴘsᴇᴅ ᴛᴜɴɴᴇʟ, there is little anyone can do except wait for the arrival of the emergency services. It is usually firefighters, with their long ladders and lifting and cutting equipment, who deal with such a rescue, but sometimes specialist engineers help to free trapped people. Failure in machinery such as cable-cars and roller-coasters can leave passengers stranded far from the ground, unable to reach safety without assistance. Disused buildings, mines, and tunnels are even more dangerous. Over time, such structures may deteriorate and become hazardous to anyone foolish enough to venture inside.

LEFT DANGLING
When a cable-car system breaks down, people are left suspended hundreds of metres up in the air. Most cable-cars have an emergency escape hatch, which may have a ladder that can be dropped to the ground.

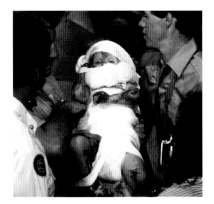

BABY JESSICA
In October 1987, 18-month-old Jessica McClure fell 6.5 m (22 ft) down a dry, abandoned well in Midland, Texas, USA. An adult could not fit down the 20-cm (8-in) wide well shaft, so rescuers drilled a vertical shaft parallel to the well, then bored a horizontal tunnel through solid rock to reach the trapped baby, who was not badly hurt.

MINE COLLAPSE
Even with sophisticated safety devices such as steel support arches and hydraulic jacks, mines are very dangerous places. Drilling into a weak spot in the rock can set off a rock-fall that could block off the route to the outside. These rescue workers are carrying a wounded man out of a gold mine after he was trapped 2,000 m (6,500 ft) underground.

FALLEN TREE
The force of a violent storm can shake even a large tree until it comes crashing down, blocking a road or falling onto a building or vehicle. Rescue crews use a huge crane to winch the tree carefully out of the way without causing further damage.

ROLLER-COASTER
The thrill of a roller-coaster ride comes from the fear that you may fall out at any moment. When the ride is in progress, passengers are held in the cars by forces created by the speed and spinning movement. However, if the roller-coaster breaks down, riders may be left hanging by their safety belts until rescuers can free them.

Visitors to an amusement park observe the scene of the accident

Cars from a funfair ride dive off the tracks

BOMB DAMAGE
A massive bomb exploded
outside the Murrah Federal Building in Oklahoma
City, USA, in April 1995, blowing up half of the nine-storey
structure. For nearly two weeks, rescue workers with trained
dogs searched the wrecked building for trapped survivors. A
day-care centre and a Social Security office were in the worst hit
part of the building. More than 80 people died in the explosion.

Air ambulances

IN MANY LARGE cities, helicopter ambulances fly high above traffic congestion and can reach a casualty more quickly than conventional road ambulances. Helicopter ambulances are also used in areas of wilderness or rough terrain that road vehicles cannot easily reach. By following detailed instructions from the ground-control crew, the pilot is able to land the helicopter as close as possible to the person who is critically ill, perhaps using the roof of a building or a clear area such as a playing field. The paramedics on board then rush to the casualty's side to give life-saving first aid. Paramedics have to complete intensive training in many aspects of medical treatment because they are usually the first to arrive at the scene of an accident, and they must work without a doctor in difficult conditions.

FLYING TO THE RESCUE
Some modern air ambulances provide a satellite screen link, enabling the paramedics to communicate with doctors at a nearby hospital. If time permits, it is often useful to consult a specialist before administering medical treatment.

INSIDE THE AIR AMBULANCE
The medical equipment carried inside the helicopter ambulance is specially designed to be light and easy to transport. Paramedics wear a protective helmet ready for work in hazardous situations.

Elasticated leg strap to secure splint

FRACTURES
Splints are used to immobilize long-bone fractures, especially in casualties with a broken leg.

Adjustable traction splint

Ankle strap to fix splint in place

Head support

Belt to secure casualty in place

BACK BOARD
Paramedics carefully transfer a patient who may have suffered a spinal injury onto a special back board, which they then carry inside the air ambulance.

FLYING DOCTORS
In parts of Africa and Australia, the distances between hospitals are so great and there are so few roads that people depend on a flying doctor to come to them when they need emergency medical treatment. A call to the nearest emergency centre brings a doctor in a light aircraft equipped to care for the patient and transfer him or her to the nearest hospital for treatment.

G-SUSX

Oxygen mask can be connected to oxygen cylinder

Suction tube placed in casualty's mouth

Mobile phone

Aspirator uses suction to clear casualty's mouth

Fluid replacement pack for patients who have lost a lot of blood

Giving set for administering fluid

Drugs for pain relief

Sterile dressing

Scissors

Stethoscope

Drugs for treating cardiac arrest

Airways enable patient to breathe

Blood-pressure meter to be strapped to patient's wrist

Pulse oxymeter to check patient's pulse

Adjustable neck collar prevents patient's head from moving until doctors can perform a thorough examination

PARAMEDIC'S "GO BAG"
All air-ambulance paramedics carry a rucksack, known as a "go bag", containing essential first-aid equipment for treating patients with a range of life-threatening conditions. Speed is vital, so the paramedics grab their bags and dash to the scene of the incident to treat the casualty as quickly as possible.

Contents of paramedic's rucksack

Ambulance equipment

THE AMBULANCE IS KITTED OUT for every kind of accident or medical emergency. There is life-saving equipment such as oxygen and drugs, bandages and splints to stop bleeding and immobilize injuries, and stretchers and blankets to make the patient comfortable. The ambulance crew decides on the correct treatment for the casualty's injuries and, if necessary, performs life-saving techniques such as cardiac massage. They stabilize the patient's condition, treating wounds and giving pain-killing drugs, then contact the hospital to tell the medical staff when they expect to arrive and to describe the patient's condition.

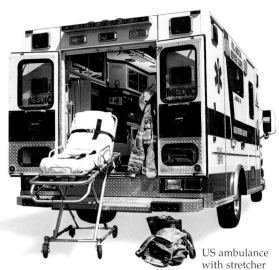

US ambulance with stretcher

STRETCHERS
Most ambulance stretchers have legs on wheels that automatically drop down to form a trolley when removed from the vehicle. The trolley can easily be lowered when it is pushed back inside the ambulance. Guard rails and straps hold the casualty in place, and the height, incline, and knee and back rests can all be adjusted to suit the patient's condition.

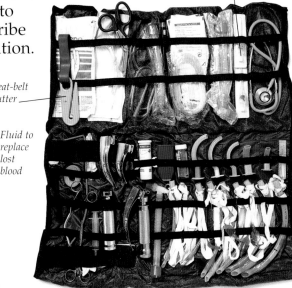

Cannula for injecting drugs

Tubes to deliver fluid into patient's bloodstream

Seat-belt cutter

Fluid to replace lost blood

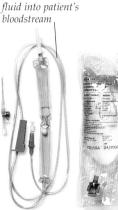

REPLACING LOST FLUID
All ambulance crews in the UK carry 2 litres (3 pints) of fluid containing vital components normally present in a person's blood. These packs are used to replace the fluid part of the blood that a casualty has lost.

INTUBATION ROLL
The crew carries a roll of equipment for treating patients with a range of conditions. Laryngoscopes are used for examining the throat, and endotracheal tubes provide a guaranteed airway for a person with severe injuries to the head or neck. The roll also holds equipment such as a stethoscope for listening to a patient's chest.

PAIN RELIEF
All casualties with serious injuries need an effective form of pain relief. The ambulance is equipped with a cylinder of gas and air, which is administered through a mask that fits over the person's mouth and nose.

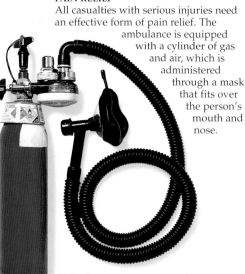

Cylinder containing gas and air

Screen displays information about the heart's rhythm

RESTARTING THE HEART
Ambulances in many countries are equipped with a cardiac defibrillator machine (left), which is used to start the heart beating again after it stops during a cardiac arrest. The machine passes an electrical current through the chest to shock the heart back into a regular rhythm.

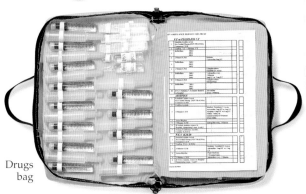

Drugs bag

CARDIAC DRUGS
The drugs bag contains adrenalin for injecting into a person who has suffered a cardiac arrest. The ambulance crew gives injections at regular intervals, and the cardiac defibrillator is used at the same time to monitor the patient's condition.

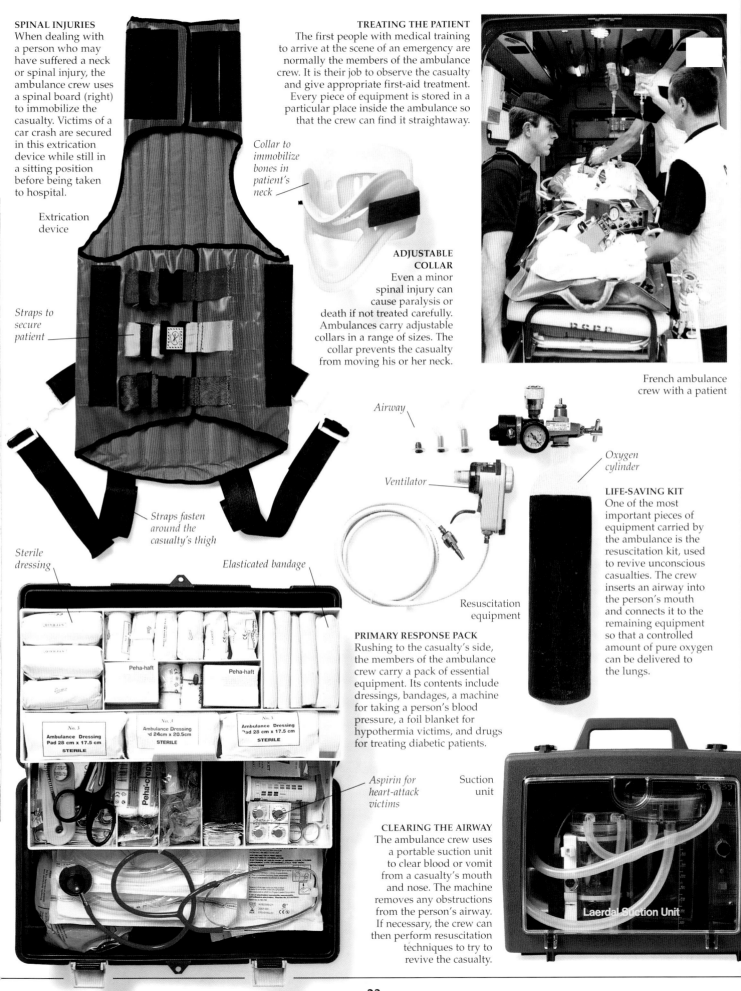

SPINAL INJURIES
When dealing with a person who may have suffered a neck or spinal injury, the ambulance crew uses a spinal board (right) to immobilize the casualty. Victims of a car crash are secured in this extrication device while still in a sitting position before being taken to hospital.

Extrication device

Collar to immobilize bones in patient's neck

Straps to secure patient

Straps fasten around the casualty's thigh

TREATING THE PATIENT
The first people with medical training to arrive at the scene of an emergency are normally the members of the ambulance crew. It is their job to observe the casualty and give appropriate first-aid treatment. Every piece of equipment is stored in a particular place inside the ambulance so that the crew can find it straightaway.

ADJUSTABLE COLLAR
Even a minor spinal injury can cause paralysis or death if not treated carefully. Ambulances carry adjustable collars in a range of sizes. The collar prevents the casualty from moving his or her neck.

French ambulance crew with a patient

Airway

Ventilator

Oxygen cylinder

Resuscitation equipment

LIFE-SAVING KIT
One of the most important pieces of equipment carried by the ambulance is the resuscitation kit, used to revive unconscious casualties. The crew inserts an airway into the person's mouth and connects it to the remaining equipment so that a controlled amount of pure oxygen can be delivered to the lungs.

Sterile dressing

Elasticated bandage

Peha-haft

Peha-haft

No. 3 Ambulance Dressing Pad 28 cm x 17.5 cm STERILE

No. 3 Ambulance Dressing ʼd 24cm x 20.5cm STERILE

No. 3 Ambulance Dressing Pad 28 cm x 17.5 cm STERILE

Peha-crep

PRIMARY RESPONSE PACK
Rushing to the casualty's side, the members of the ambulance crew carry a pack of essential equipment. Its contents include dressings, bandages, a machine for taking a person's blood pressure, a foil blanket for hypothermia victims, and drugs for treating diabetic patients.

Aspirin for heart-attack victims

Suction unit

CLEARING THE AIRWAY
The ambulance crew uses a portable suction unit to clear blood or vomit from a casualty's mouth and nose. The machine removes any obstructions from the person's airway. If necessary, the crew can then perform resuscitation techniques to try to revive the casualty.

Laerdal Suction Unit

Emergency medicine

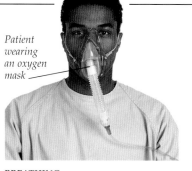

BREATHING
One of the body's vital functions is respiration (breathing). As a person breathes in air, the body extracts the oxygen that it needs. When a patient is struggling to breathe, a member of the medical staff covers his or her mouth and nose with a mask attached to a cylinder of pure oxygen.

THE BUSIEST PART OF ANY HOSPITAL is the emergency department. As an ambulance arrives, paramedics fling open the vehicle's doors and wheel the patient inside, describing the person's condition to the first doctor to appear. The priority for the emergency team is to save the patient's life by regulating vital body functions. This could mean restarting the heart, clearing the airway to help the person breathe, giving drugs to reverse an allergic reaction, or attending to severe wounds. In some situations, the team can only try to stabilize a patient's body functions before rushing him or her to an operating theatre for surgery. Recent advances in equipment, drugs, and surgical techniques mean that medical emergencies that would have been fatal 50 years ago can now be treated successfully.

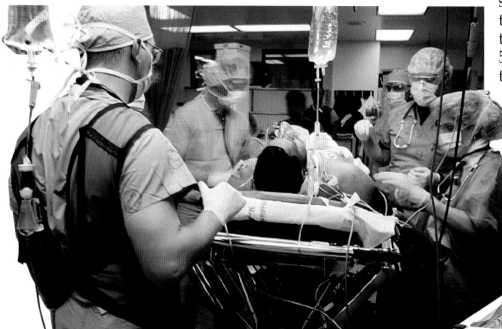

IN THE EMERGENCY DEPARTMENT
As paramedics wheel the ambulance trolley into the emergency department, the team of doctors and nurses swiftly responds to information about the injury or illness that the patient is suffering. The team then prepares to perform whatever procedures are necessary to save the patient's life.

Balloon to pump air into patient while waiting for oxygen supply

CRASH TROLLEY
When a life-threatening emergency occurs, staff rush a hospital crash trolley to the patient's bedside. The trolley contains equipment to deal with a huge variety of situations, from a cardiac arrest (when the heart stops beating) to an intense allergic reaction. Each item is placed in a standard position on the trolley so that medical staff can find it quickly and easily.

Print-out to show rhythm of the heart

Drug boxes containing heart stimulants and other drugs

Fluid products, tubes, and needles

Hospital emergency trolley

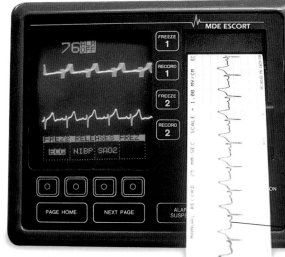

SCREENING THE BODY
Sometimes, doctors need to look inside a patient's body to detect a medical problem. Scans are used to examine soft tissues, while X-rays reveal broken bones. An ECG (electrocardiograph), shown above, monitors heart disorders by detecting electrical signals produced by the heart as it beats.

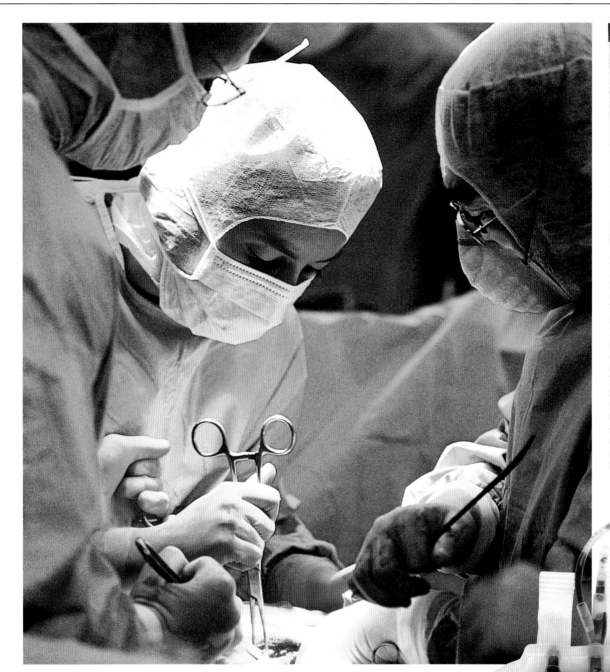

REHYDRATION SALTS
Dehydration is one of the most common medical emergencies dealt with by charity workers in developing countries. It is often caused by an outbreak of typhoid or cholera, which may lead to diarrhoea. A dehydrated body loses so many natural fluids and minerals that the person's life is put at risk. Rehydration salts containing minerals such as potassium, sodium, and sugar, added to water are an effective remedy.

A team of surgeons performing open-heart surgery

VITAL SURGERY
When a patient's injury or illness is so severe that it is necessary to cut him or her open to repair or remove body parts, surgery must take place as soon as possible. With modern equipment and advanced techniques, surgeons can keep a patient alive even while repairing major organs such as the heart and lungs.

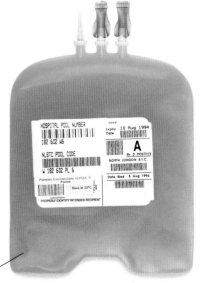

LIFE BLOOD
Patients who have lost a lot of blood require a transfusion directly into their bloodstream. Healthy people donate blood for use in emergencies, and it is stored in a blood bank. Sometimes rather than whole blood, blood plasma is used. This is the fluid part that contains salts, sugars, proteins involved in blood clotting, and antibodies used in fighting infections.

Platelets to help blood clot

Bag of concentrated red blood cells

The police force

French national
police force badge

IN AN EMERGENCY, spotting a uniformed police officer approaching the scene comes as a great relief. He or she will take control of the situation and notify whichever emergency services are needed by radio. The police officer will also keep onlookers and passing vehicles at a distance from the scene. To control violent situations, police officers may carry a stick, a CS gas spray, or, in some cases, a gun. As well as regular officers, many forces have teams to assist with search and rescue operations, particularly in areas such as national parks where people often become lost. Other specialist teams, such as mounted police, dog handlers, and helicopter crews, can be called in to handle a variety of situations.

POLICE CAR
Distinctive livery with reflective markings and a prominent badge makes police cars easy to distinguish from other vehicles on the road.

Flashing light

PATROL BIKE
As well as manoeuvring through traffic that would delay a larger vehicle, a police motorbike can speed down alleys and over rough terrain where a car cannot go. In some areas, motorbikes similar to those designed for cross-country racing are used to assist in mountain or wilderness rescue operations.

Greek traffic
police officer

Riot helmet

DIRECTING TRAFFIC
Police officers direct traffic away from the scene of an accident and control roads when they become dangerously crowded. Officers may use whistles to attract the attention of drivers, and wear white or reflective gloves to make their gestures clear.

Jacket with reflective strips for improved visibility in the dark

Protective visor

ON HORSEBACK
Sitting high above the ground, a mounted officer can watch for trouble in a crowd and reach anyone in need of assistance quickly. In a riot, a mounted officer and his or her horse, both protected by riot gear, can stand up to attack more easily than an officer on foot.

Leg guard

SEARCHING WITH DOGS
Police dogs are trained to help find missing people, using their acute sense of smell to follow the scent track left by the person. Each dog is trained and cared for by its own handler, and the two build up a close relationship. Police dogs are also trained to chase criminals and grab them by the arm to prevent them from escaping. The German shepherd is the breed of dog most often used by police forces.

A VIEW FROM ABOVE
Run jointly by the police and ambulance service, this helicopter's crew of three includes a pilot, a police officer, and a paramedic. Helicopters can cover a wide area in a search and rescue operation far more quickly than officers on foot or in cars. Using the heat-sensing camera on the front, the crew can locate missing people and suspected offenders even in darkness or bad weather.

Heat-sensing camera

Moving map display

Video/ infra-red control panel

INSIDE THE COCKPIT
A "sky shout" system in the helicopter's cockpit enables the crew to call out to people on the ground or emit a siren. Other state-of-the-art equipment includes a global positioning system (GPS) with a moving map display to show the pilot the helicopter's precise location and guide it to the exact spot where it is needed.

CONTROLLING THE SCENE
At the scene of a road traffic accident, a fire, or other serious emergency, police officers stop or divert traffic, then cordon off the road with plastic tape or traffic cones. This helps the other emergency services to tackle the situation and remove injured people speedily. It also stops other people or vehicles from approaching the scene before it is safe.

Maintenance vehicle arrives to clear the road

Police officers organize the removal of a crashed vehicle

Armed-response teams

SAS BADGE
The British army's secret regiment, the Special Air Service (SAS), has the motto "Who dares wins".

Foresight

A TERRORIST BURSTS INTO an aeroplane's cockpit shouting "There's a bomb on board, do exactly what I tell you!", or bank robbers draw their weapons and yell "Get down on the floor!", and at once teams of armed police officers or soldiers are called in. Where possible, specially trained personnel first try to negotiate with the aggressors. It is a tense situation. The terrorists or criminals are surrounded by armed personnel, so they cannot escape. But their strength is that while they hold hostages, the forces around them do not want to attack for fear of injuring innocent people. As soon as negotiations break down or hostages begin to be harmed, the waiting armed-response teams spring into action to bring the incident to an end.

STORMING THE IRANIAN EMBASSY
In April 1980, terrorists broke into the Iranian Embassy in London, England. When they killed two hostages, the SAS prepared to attack. Some of the team swung down from ropes attached to the roof and broke in using sledgehammers and explosives. They rescued the hostages six days after the start of the siege.

Commando unit in training, El Salvador

TRAINING
As well as undergoing tough physical training, members of an armed-response squad may learn to survive and operate in different environments such as deserts, mountains, jungles, and at sea. They acquire all kinds of special skills such as new languages, advanced first aid, Morse code, parachuting, and dealing with weapons and explosives.

SWAT TEAMS
The armed-response units of the US police service are called SWAT (Special Weapons and Tactics) teams. They are vital when a situation goes beyond the control of ordinary police officers, such as during a siege. This SWAT team member is moving in to enable a cornered gunman to talk to negotiators.

Nightsight

Adjustable
butt

MP5 sub-
machine gun

Balaclava

Gas mask

SAS UNIFORM

Body armour protects members of armed-response teams against bullets, knives, and physical attacks. During some operations, they wear balaclavas to make themselves unrecognizable. Soldiers may use gas masks during a raid as protection against toxic gas and fumes from stun grenades.

WEAPONS

Members of these teams are armed with light but accurate weapons, which are easy to handle even in challenging circumstances. They are also trained to use explosives and a variety of other weapons that they might capture from an enemy.

Leather glove

Body armour

HIJACK

In order to achieve goals such as the release of political prisoners, terrorists may take over an aeroplane by force and hold the passengers and crew hostage. Negotiators and armed-response teams are called in to attempt to release the hostages and capture the hijackers.

Magazine
pouch

Thigh strap

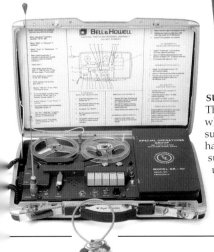

SURVEILLANCE

The most important preparation when dealing with a situation such as a hijack is to know what is happening through close surveillance. This can be done using binoculars, phone taps, bugs, or other listening devices, such as those in this police audio-surveillance briefcase used in the 1960s and 1970s.

Reinforced
toe-cap

Lifeguards

ON A CROWDED BEACH or in a swimming pool, it can be difficult to tell the difference between someone jumping and waving in high spirits and a person in serious trouble. Danger can strike at any moment, as people swim or drift too far out or get caught by dangerous currents or huge waves. They may be overcome by cramp or sudden illness, hit their head on a rock, or fall prey to jellyfish stings or even shark attacks. But lifeguards patrolling the beach or pool are ready to dive in to rescue anyone in trouble. These expert swimmers are trained to bring people safely to dry land and give emergency first aid.

ON THE LOOKOUT
From a high point like this lookout tower on a beach in Hawaii, a lifeguard can keep watch over a wide section of the water even if the beach is crowded. Lifeguards use binoculars to help them scan the sea as far as the horizon.

TRAINED LIFEGUARDS
This sign shows that there is a professional lifeguard on duty, able to give advice on the state of the water as well as rescue people in trouble.

OCEAN SAFETY
LIFEGUARD
CITY & COUNTY OF HONOLULU

ROWING TO THE RESCUE
The high surf around some Australian beaches catches many people unawares. Danger areas are equipped with large rowing boats, which can be crewed by several lifeguards. The boats are specially designed to ride over the huge waves without capsizing. A lifeguard in waters like these must be an extremely strong swimmer, able to cope with strong currents and giant waves while rescuing another person.

WARNING SIGNS
On popular swimming and surfing beaches, permanent notices warn of dangers such as strong currents or high surf.

ON THE BEACH
Once a lifeguard has brought a casualty safely to shore, he or she carries out simple first-aid treatment. This may involve laying the person in a recovery position to expel water from the lungs. The lifeguard may also perform mouth-to-mouth resuscitation or bind up wounds. If necessary, the patient can then be rushed to hospital.

A green flag means that it is safe to swim

SWIMMING SAFELY

At the edge of guarded sections of a beach, coloured flags are posted each day to indicate the condition of the water.

HEAD ABOVE WATER

When rescuing someone in trouble in the water, it is vital to keep his or her head above water while swimming to safety. This prevents the victim from swallowing or breathing in any water. The rescuer needs to have a firm grip, as a drowning person often struggles and can endanger both of them.

Rescuer with arm around person's chest

Safety helmet

Rescuer holds oar firmly

Victim holds on with both hands until he is hauled in

REACHING OUT

If someone falls into deep water such as a swimming pool, harbour, or lake, or from a boat on calm water such as a river or canal, it may be possible to rescue him or her without entering the water. The rescuer can hold out an oar, a long pole, or a similar object for the person in the water to grab hold of and then pull him or her to safety.

RIDING INTO TROUBLE

In many holiday resorts, small, fast jet skis with engines the size of mopeds have become popular. However, holidaymakers can hire these craft with little or no training, and inexperienced riders manoeuvring them around waters crowded with bathers have caused accidents to themselves and other people. This places extra demands on the busy lifeguard service.

Coastal rescue

W HEN A MAYDAY CALL from a vessel in distress reaches the lifeboat station, the crew springs into action. Some rescue craft are moored by the station, while others slide down a slipway into the sea. As they speed to the scene, the crew members keep in touch with the damaged vessel and other rescue services by radio. Air and sea rescue teams work closely together in coastal areas. Helicopters quickly carry victims out of danger, but lifeboat crews can rescue injured sailors and deal with damaged boats more effectively.

OUT IN ALL WEATHERS
Heavy seas present few problems for an all-weather lifeboat. If the boat capsizes, it will automatically right itself. This type of craft can operate in waters as shallow as 2 m (6 ft) or rush to rescues up to 80 km (50 miles) out to sea at a top speed of 33 km/h (21 mph). It can bring up to 78 survivors back to shore.

Rope carrying strap

Straps for securing casualty

STRETCHER
Specially adapted stretchers are needed to support casualties who may be suffering from broken limbs or spines.

Headrest

Boat hook

Bilge pump

Speedline device

Life jacket

ESSENTIAL EQUIPMENT
The lifeboat is kitted out for every eventuality. This hand-operated bilge pump drains water out of boats that are in trouble so that they float higher in the water. Rescuers use boat hooks to pull small craft or people in the water towards the lifeboat. If someone has drifted further away, the speedline device can fire a line of rope as far as 230 m (755 ft). The crew throws life jackets to keep people afloat until they can be rescued.

SMALL AND SPEEDY
For rescue operations close to the shore, such as rescues from cliffs or from a dinghy that has drifted too far, a rigid inflatable boat (RIB), is used. These boats can work close to rocks and in shallow water without running aground and move at a top speed of 54 km/h (33 mph).

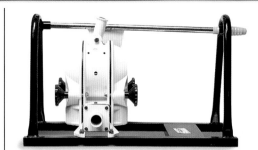

Inflatable airbag used to right the craft if it overturns

Safety helmet

Control panel operated by helmsman

Lifeline for survivors in the water to grab

Radar reflector

PHYL CLARE 3

B-746

RNLI

Plastic hull

*Pilot can alter
the angle of the
rotor blades to
change direction*

*Winch is
controlled by the
winch operator
inside the helicopter*

*Sponson stabilizes
the helicopter if it
lands on water*

HM COASTGUARD

RESCUE

UP, UP, AND AWAY

Helicopters can travel greater distances
than lifeboats, so they are mainly used
for rescues far out at sea. They are also
ideal in situations where a lifeboat is
hindered by dangerous rocks. The
helicopter hovers above the scene and
lowers a winchman to rescue survivors.
The lifeboat and helicopter services also
co-operate for rescues close to shore,
with the helicopter collecting
injured passengers and
speeding them to hospital.

*Flotation bag
in case of an
emergency
landing
on water*

*Main wheels retract
into the sponson
during flight*

*Floodlight
illuminates
rescue scenes
during night-
time operations*

*A steel cable
allows the
winchman to
descend as far as
75 m (245 ft)
if necessary*

*The winchman
attaches a hook to the
survivor and supports
him with his legs*

FINDING SURVIVORS

Modern lifeboats carry a
range of hi-tech equipment
to help the crew find any
trouble spot without delay.
As they race to the scene,
the crew keeps in contact
with the vessel that is in
trouble, and with other
rescue services whose help
may be needed. Crew
members are trained in
plotting their course on
a map and in the use of
sophisticated radio and
navigation equipment,
such as radar screens.

FIREBOATS

When a fire breaks out near a harbour or on a boat that
has docked, rescuers call in a fireboat. With an endless
supply of water to pump from, a fireboat can discharge
about 34,000 litres (9,000 gallons) of water per second –
five times more than a large fire engine. The boat is also
equipped with tanks of foam to tackle oil-based fires.

Ocean rescue

A STORM AT SEA can last for days, with giant waves lashing the decks and the wind tossing ships around like playthings. But even a badly damaged vessel can provide shelter, water, and food, as well as life-saving equipment and a radio, so the safest place to be is on board. If the boat capsizes, people adrift in heavy seas are likely to drown before help arrives. A calm sea can be almost as hazardous, as cold and fatigue soon numb the bodies of those floating for too long. A vessel in distress sends out regular radio messages to other ships that may be passing and to the nearest coastguard station. When it becomes too dangerous to stay on board, the captain gives the signal to abandon ship. People head for lifeboats, taking with them survival equipment, food, and fresh water.

Foghorn

Emergency flares

TO THE RESCUE
British sailor Pete Goss had just battled through a hurricane in the Southern Ocean during the 1996/7 round-the-world solo yacht race when he heard a distress call. Goss turned back into the storm to rescue fellow competitor, Frenchman Raphael Dinelli, who was clinging desperately to a life raft.

NOT A DROP TO DRINK
Adrift in an ocean full of water that they cannot drink because it is too salty, people are more likely to suffer from dehydration than any other ailment. Most life rafts are equipped with bags of fresh drinking water that must be carefully rationed amongst those on board until help arrives.

HERE WE ARE!
People on board a vessel that is in trouble send emergency flares high into the sky to guide a rescue craft to their exact location. A foghorn makes an ear-piercing noise that alerts other vessels to a ship's presence, even in darkness or bad weather.

LIFE-SAVER
Life buoys are kept on the decks of ships so that rescuers can throw them to people in distress in the water. The buoys are made of a ring of cork covered with canvas, and the rope makes them easier to grasp, helping a person to stay afloat without struggling.

Seven Oceans
DRINKING WATER
TRINKWASSER · EAU POTABLE
AGUA POTABLE · DRIKKEVANN

SIGNALLING DISTRESS
Signal flags were flown from the masts of ships to pass messages to nearby vessels for centuries before the invention of the radio, and the system is still in use today. Certain flags convey a specific meaning when used alone, or more precise messages can be spelled out using a combination of flags.

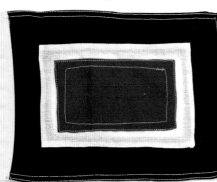

I am on fire; keep clear of me

I require medical assistance

ICEBERG ALERT
Special design features were thought to have made the *Titanic* unsinkable, so lifeboats were only supplied for half of the passengers. However, on its maiden voyage in April 1912, an iceberg ripped a gash in the side of the ship, and it began to sink. Wireless operators tapped out distress messages to ships in the area, but by the time the *Carpathia* came to the rescue only 706 people remained alive out of the 2,223 on board.

Ventilation and observation tube

INFLATABLE LIFE RAFT
Seagoing vessels must carry sufficient small boats to accommodate all the people on board. Designed to stay afloat in the roughest seas, these rescue craft range from large rigid lifeboats to small inflatable dinghies. Many are equipped with emergency tools and provisions and a canopy to protect those inside from exposure to fierce sun, cold winds, or driving rain.

Man overboard

Four-person life raft

Mountain rescue

Rescue post sign

A WALK ON A GENTLE mountain slope can seem safe in warm sunshine, but if fog suddenly descends, badly equipped walkers may become lost and even wander onto more dangerous parts of the mountain. Mountaineers have better training and are equipped to deal with emergencies, but accidents still happen. Skiing can also be dangerous, and broken limbs are a common occurrence. Skiing off the controlled "piste" areas is extremely risky, as there may be hazards under the snow, or loose snow that could turn into an avalanche. The greatest danger on a mountain is caused by the weather. Rescue services are often called out in severe conditions such as avalanches, dense fog, blizzards, and rainstorms.

TRAINED TEAMS
Most popular skiing and mountaineering resorts have teams of professional rescuers, while in other areas volunteers are on call. Rescue teams must know the terrain very well and have first-aid training. They also work closely with other services. The team takes its vehicles as close as possible to where they are needed, then unloads its equipment and continues on foot.

Roof cage for large equipment

Radio aerial

AVALANCHE
On a steep, snow-covered mountainside, a gust of wind, a loud noise, or a sudden movement may set off an avalanche of snow, ice, and rock debris, which can fly down a slope at 320 km/h (200 mph), making escape impossible. In winter, fresh snow may slide off older, compacted layers, while spring thaws can cause the entire mass of snow to slip.

Winch

CLIMBING EQUIPMENT

A rescue team may need to scale steep, icy slopes or climb into narrow crevices to rescue people who have fallen. Climbing equipment including ropes, ladders, and ice axes is essential for this type of rescue.

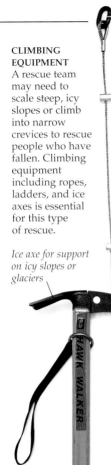

Ice axe for support on icy slopes or glaciers

THE POWER OF SNOW

The strength of an avalanche can be enormously destructive, felling trees and crushing buildings in its path. In populated areas where roads or buildings lie in the possible path of an avalanche, safety experts may start controlled mini-avalanches to dislodge unstable masses of snow and stop the build-up of bigger avalanches.

Stainless-steel ladder

Stretchable nylon rope

RESCUE FROM THE AIR

Helicopters are the quickest and most effective means of lifting an injured person from a mountain or dropping a search party in a likely location. Sometimes, specially trained dogs are lowered to find people lost in the snow. However, helicopters cannot be used in fierce winds, heavy snow, or thick clouds, or if there is a chance of the rotor blades disturbing the snow and starting an avalanche.

Air rescue

Mᴏsᴛ ᴀɪʀ ᴅɪsᴀsᴛᴇʀs are caused by bad weather, pilot error, or mechanical failure. The most dangerous accidents happen on take-off when the fuel tanks are full of flammable aviation fuel. A vital part of a pilot's training is learning how to react in any emergency. This training is carried out in a flight simulator, which sits on hydraulic support jacks that give a very realistic impression of movement, while images are screened in front of the pilot and sounds are played. When a plane crash or a forced landing occurs, the aircraft's crew are trained to keep people as safe as possible and take care of them until rescue teams arrive. Sometimes, it is difficult for rescue services to locate the survivors, either because radio contact has been lost, or if the pilot has been killed, the crew may not know exactly where they are.

JUNGLE LANDING
In 1989, a Boeing 737 from São Paulo, Brazil, ran out of fuel over the Amazon jungle. The pilot was forced to land on the tops of trees. The branches cushioned the landing and 41 of the 54 people on board survived. When rescuers reached them four days later, they were suffering only from thirst, insect bites, and bee-stings.

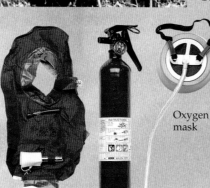

Life jacket

Fire-extinguisher

Oxygen mask

PASSENGER PROTECTION
Aircraft are fitted with many safety devices to deal with problems such as a loss of air pressure, emergency landings, and fires. All passengers are supplied with life jackets under their seats and oxygen masks that drop down from overhead panels. Rapidly inflating dinghies can be thrown out for use in emergency sea landings.

Heat-reflecting suit

PROTECTIVE CLOTHING
Airport firefighters wear special clothing to protect them from intense flames and smoke. This member of a US fire crew is wearing a fire-retardant suit and breathing apparatus. Crews train for all kinds of emergencies that may take place in real life.

General-purpose line (rope)

Fire blanket

Fog gun for discharging water

SPECIAL ATTACHMENTS
The attachments fitted on the end of the fire hoses are called branches. Firefighters can choose from different types, depending on the nature of the fire.

Aspirated foam branch for dealing with aviation fuel fires

Fire-extinguisher

Tool kit

CRASH LANDING

In 1996, Ethiopian Airways flight ET 961 was hijacked 15 minutes after leaving Addis Ababa, the country's capital. The pilot battled with the hijackers for control of the aircraft, then managed to crash-land the plane in shallow water 300 m (330 yds) from a beach off the Comoros Islands in the Indian Ocean. Holiday-makers swam out to sea to rescue the survivors.

Inflatable airbag used by airport firefighters

AIRBAGS

These large airbags can be used to support damaged aircraft on the ground. Wedged under the wing of a crashed plane, a bag can be filled with air, raising the wing so that rescue services can reach the worst affected parts.

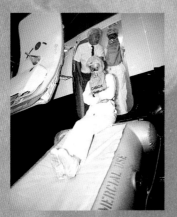

DOWN THE CHUTE

The doorways of passenger aircraft are equipped with inflatable chutes for passengers to slide down in the event of an emergency landing. Tests show that planes can be cleared of passengers in minutes if everyone follows the crew's evacuation instructions. However, passengers often cause delays by stopping to collect their belongings.

TEAM ON THE SCENE

When a crash or a fire occurs at an airport, air traffic control alerts the airport's own fire crew with a bell that rings in the fire station. A fire truck like this one can reach any part of the airport within three minutes. Most trucks carry their own water supply, since the incident may be some distance from a water source. Firefighters can target the heart of the blaze using the monitor (water cannon) on the roof of the truck.

Warning light

Stem lights for illuminating work in the dark

Triple extension ladder

Blue flashing light

Monitor can shoot a jet of water or foam

Inlet for plugging hose into mains water hydrant

International aid

W HEN A DISASTER such as famine, flood, drought, or war affects the welfare of the people of a whole country, rescue teams from around the world arrive quickly to deal with the emergency. Basic humanitarian needs, such as food, clean water, health care, and a safe place to stay, are provided first. Then aid agencies provide seeds, building materials, and other necessities to help people reconstruct their lives. Some aid is provided by the governments of other countries, but much is supplied by non-governmental aid agencies, such as the Red Cross and Médecins Sans Frontières, staffed mainly by volunteers and funded by donations. Even those agencies that have a religious background, such as Christian Aid, try to be independent from religious, political, and economic influences. Assistance from a foreign government is more likely to be affected by the opinions of that country, for example helping only one side in a conflict.

People wait for food in a refugee camp, Sudan, 1991

FAMINE RELIEF
In the hottest, driest parts of the world, every drop of rain is vital if crops are to grow. When a drought strikes, crops fail, food stores run out, and people begin to starve. Poor, drought-stricken countries turn to international aid agencies to provide and distribute food and clean water to wherever they are needed.

THE RED CROSS
After a tsunami (tidal wave) hit Papua New Guinea in 1997, clean drinking water was in short supply. The Red Cross dug wells, so that women had access to water without having to trek all day to fetch it. The Red Cross was founded in 1863 to care for war casualties but today provides humanitarian aid in all sorts of international emergencies.

Clearing landmines in Cambodia

LANDMINES
Even after the end of a war, landmines laid during the conflict can still kill and maim people, so they have to be carefully removed. International organizations, such as the Halo Trust, clear the landmines and dispose of them so that people can return to their daily lives without the risk of injury.

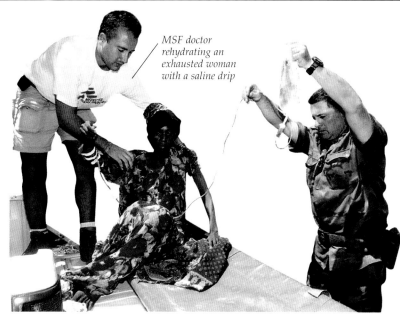

MSF doctor rehydrating an exhausted woman with a saline drip

PEACE-KEEPING

Formed in 1945 to maintain international peace, the United Nations is funded by the world's governments, and most countries are members. When a conflict breaks out or a threat of war arises, the UN sends in troops to protect civilians by trying to re-establish peace or prevent the war. UN troops wear blue helmets and patrol the country in specially marked vehicles.

DOCTORS WITHOUT BORDERS

When any emergency occurs – famine, flood, armed conflict, natural disaster, or epidemic – rescue teams from Médecins Sans Frontières, the world's largest medical relief organization, are among the first to arrive. Here a doctor from MSF cares for a woman who had to flee her home after terrible flooding in Mozambique in March 2000.

A PLACE OF SAFETY

Refugees, like these exhausted Tsutsi people in war-torn Rwanda in 1984, are forced from their homes by a natural disaster, such as a flood or famine, or driven out by war or persecution. Organizations such as the Red Cross and the UN set up camps where refugees can remain until they are able to return home or new homes can be found.

Refugees carry their belongings and search for a safe place to stay

Animals to the rescue

HIGHLY INTELLIGENT, easy to train, and equipped with a superb sense of smell, dogs form a vital part of many rescue teams. In the 1600s, monks in the Swiss Alps began to use St Bernard dogs to rescue people buried in snowdrifts. During World War II, dogs proved their worth again by sniffing out people trapped in rubble after bombing raids.

St Bernard dog

The success of these dogs has inspired their use today in the search for survivors of avalanches and earthquakes. However, other animals may also take part in rescue operations. Sometimes animals are chosen for particular characteristics, such as the homing pigeons used to pass messages in wartime. Perhaps the bravest of all are the heroic pets who risk their own lives to save their owners from danger.

Miniature parachute canopy to provide a soft landing for the bird

Lightweight string attaches parachute to bird

Padded corselet to protect bird

PIGEON AT WAR
In times of war, pigeons are able to carry life-saving information though bombs and gunfire when no other means of communication is available. During World War II, pigeons were dropped by parachute to British spies in France. The birds flew home at speeds of more than 145 km/h (90 mph) with secret messages in containers attached to their legs.

BURIED IN THE SNOW
When an avalanche has occurred, rescue teams with dogs search for survivors buried in the snow. With its acute sense of smell, a single dog can search a wide area in the time that it would take 20 people to complete the same task. Dog breeds used for these searches are usually German shepherds, labradors, or border collies.

DOLPHIN RESCUES

The extraordinary ancient tales of dolphins saving drowning people and escorting ships through perilous waters seem to contain some elements of truth. In modern times, there have been reports of dolphins pushing drowning people to the surface for air, and splashing around a person clinging to wreckage in the water, as if warning them not to fall asleep.

A rescue worker at the scene of an earthquake in Mexico City, 1985

ANIMAL WARNINGS

For thousands of years, animals have been thought to warn people of natural disasters by behaving strangely. In recent years, Chinese scientists have tried to find a method of detecting earthquakes by observing animal behaviour. In 1975, they predicted an earthquake at Haicheng when snakes woke from hibernation and rats began to swarm. Just 12 hours after the city was evacuated, it was flattened by a massive earthquake.

SEARCHING IN THE RUBBLE

This specially trained dog is sniffing for signs of survivors in the rubble of a building destroyed by an earthquake. After an earthquake or an explosion, the remains of many structures are unstable, and there may be gas leaks and broken glass. In spite of these hazards, rescue dogs are able to tread lightly over the wreckage to locate survivors.

A dog searches for survivors in the rubble

RSPCA animal medallion

ANIMAL AWARDS

Charities such as the American Humane Association, the British RSPCA, and the People's Dispensary for Sick Animals (PDSA) award medals to animals that show special bravery. Award-winners have dragged people from fires or rescued them from drowning, barked to warn their owners of dangers such as fires or gas leaks, and even detected changes in babies' breathing patterns that indicated a medical problem.

Wartime rescues

FOR SUPREME COURAGE
Governments award medals to service men and women who have risked their lives, acting with bravery beyond the call of duty.

IN WARTIME, everyone is a potential victim, and so rescue operations are continually taking place. Soldiers and civilians injured by bullets, bombs, shells, and chemicals need to be quickly evacuated to a safe place where they can receive medical treatment. People may become trapped behind enemy lines or captured and put in prisoner of war camps. Rescues from such situations may be by a swift, unexpected military attack, by a secret escape plan, or under a white flag of truce. Some of the rescue services that we take for granted in peacetime, such as ambulances, were first developed for use in times of war. The terrible wounds and diseases suffered by soldiers during conflicts have led to important medical developments, such as antibiotics to fight infection and plastic surgery for the treatment of burn victims.

DOG SOLDIERS
Dogs have been specially trained to perform a vital role on the battlefield. The dog climbs out of the trenches into no-man's land, checks bodies for signs of life, and lies beside a wounded soldier until someone is able to carry the casualty to safety. The key to a good dog soldier is the ability to stay calm even under gunfire and shelling.

THE LADY WITH THE LAMP
When Florence Nightingale (1820–1910) entered the filthy, rat-infested hospital at Scutari in Turkey during the Crimean War (1853–56), a patient's chance of dying was one in three. Within months, Nightingale and her staff of 38 nurses established a regime of fresh air, light, warmth, cleanliness, quiet, and good food, which decreased the death rate to only one in 40.

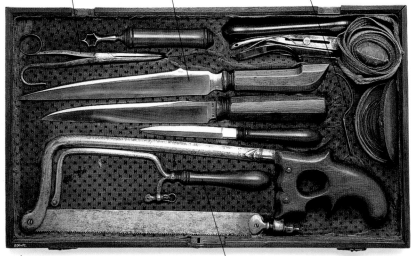

Forceps *Large knife for cutting muscle* *Suture (sewing) needle*

18th-century amputation set *Small saw for amputating fingers and toes*

PASS THE SAW!
For centuries, limbs badly damaged in combat had to be amputated before life-threatening infection set in. Amputated limbs were treated with hot pitch (a by-product of tar), then cauterized (sealed) with hot irons to stop them from bleeding. Sixteenth-century French surgeon Ambroise Paré (1510–1590) improved survival rates by replacing the pitch with ointment made from egg yolk and turpentine and by tying off exposed blood vessels rather than cauterizing.

American four-engined transport plane

BERLIN AIRLIFT
The biggest emergency air mission of all time happened after World War II. In 1948, the Soviet Union cut off all rail, road, and water links with West Berlin in order to force the Western Allied powers – the USA, the UK, and France – to abandon their rights there. For 11 months, aircraft flew into West Berlin carrying 2 million tonnes of vital supplies for the population of the city, until the blockade was eventually lifted.

BATTLEFIELD AMBULANCES
The first ambulances were simple carts for carrying stretchers, with no trained medical staff to tend to the wounded. It was during Napoleon's invasion of Italy in 1796 that French military surgeon Dominique Jean Laurey (1766–1842) first introduced these "flying ambulances" – light, fast, one-horse vehicles that dashed onto the battlefield to pick up the wounded and took them to a hospital to be treated.

World War I horse-drawn ambulance

OPERATION DYNAMO
Following the fall of France in 1940, British and French troops were trapped on the beaches around Dunkirk in the north of France by the advancing German army. More than 900 yachts, motor cruisers, barges, and cockle boats, crewed by ordinary people, sailed across the English Channel to rescue 338,000 men. Some carried troops all the way back, avoiding mines and heavy fire from low-flying aircraft. Others ferried troops to naval ships anchored further offshore.

AIR AMBULANCES
Helicopters fitted out as field hospitals with trained medical staff were first used by the US Army during the Vietnam War (1961–75). Helicopters are vital rescue vehicles in wartime because of their manoeuvrability. They can swoop down over difficult terrain where there is no landing strip available and pluck injured troops from the battlefield or rescue soldiers from behind enemy lines.

Natural disasters

Storms, blizzards, floods, landslides, tidal waves – the forces of nature can strike without warning, bringing great devastation and loss of life. In response, governments declare a disaster area or state of emergency in the affected regions and send in rescue services to control the situation. People may be killed or injured in the disaster, and many will lose their homes. Chaos may break out as services such as electricity, water, and telephones are cut off, and there may be a shortage of food, fuel, and other supplies. Most natural disasters are difficult to predict, but some regions live under threat of severe storms or floods on a regular basis. Advance planning in such areas can reduce the effects by providing protective measures, such as flood barriers or storm shelters, as well as early warning where possible.

TWISTER
Tornadoes arise suddenly and unpredictably, so in high-risk areas, such as central parts of the USA, houses are built with underground storm cellars. The best protection against a tornado is to get into a cellar or the middle of a house with as many walls between you and the outside as possible. This photograph shows a typical scene of destruction left by a mighty tornado.

VIEW FROM ABOVE
In this satellite photograph, the swirling winds around the centre of Typhoon Pat can be clearly seen. This typhoon (another name for a hurricane) struck the eastern Pacific in 1985. Scientists track the progress of these storms using sophisticated weather satellites that allow them to warn people in threatened areas a few days in advance.

SEA OF MUD
In 1985, when the Nevada del Ruiz volcano erupted in Colombia, a mudslide of snow, pumice, and ash swept through the town of Amero at speeds of up to 35 km/h (20 mph). Medical teams, firefighters, the army, air force, and international rescue experts were brought in to free survivors from the waves of mud and debris which surrounded them like wet concrete.

Helicopter airlifts a survivor to safety

WATER, WATER EVERYWHERE
Torrential rain, melting ice and snow, dam breaches, or storms at sea can cause a river to burst its banks or waves to surge over coastal land. A powerful flood smashes houses and washes away vehicles, while sewage overflows from drains. Helicopters and boats search for survivors such as these people in Mozambique, trapped on the roof of a house.

WATER BOMBS

To combat a forest fire from above, a firefighting plane scoops up water from the sea or lakes into its huge tanks, then swoops as low as 30 m (100 ft) over the flames, dropping its load. A coloured chemical may be added to the water to stop it dispersing into a fine mist and to show the pilot which areas have already been drenched.

Coloured water

WIND AND RAIN

In 1992, when Hurricane Andrew struck Miami, USA, roads were jammed with more than a million people leaving the area. Thanks to early warning given by weather forecasters, by the time the storm hit, most people were prepared, and relief agencies had set up shelters for those made homeless.

FOREST FIRES

In the hot, dry summers of areas such as southern France, southeast Australia, and California, USA, forest fires are a constant danger, threatening local people, animals, and holidaymakers. Fires may start from a lightning strike, a carelessly dropped match, or when a build-up of rotting vegetation bursts into flames. The blaze then spreads through the undergrowth and leaps from tree to tree at speeds of up to 160 km/h (100 mph).

SMOKEJUMPERS

In remote forest areas, brave firefighters called smokejumpers parachute in to suppress wildfires before they spread. Using pumps, shovels, and saws, they clear a path around the fire and fell dead trees, aiming to isolate the blaze until ground crews arrive. A smokejumper may spend up to 18 hours at a time digging fire lines, only to be forced to flee through the forest by the speed and heat of the spreading fire.

Earthquake rescue

A MASSIVE EARTHQUAKE shakes the ground, its unleashed energy toppling buildings and causing great cracks to open in the Earth's surface. Vibrations radiate out from the epicentre, gradually weakening as they travel further from the source. Survivors may be trapped for days, buried, wounded, or unconscious under the rubble. Even those who are not injured are soon in danger of dehydration, which can lead to death. As local people rush away from the disaster, rescue teams head towards it. For the rescuers, it is a race against time to find the victims and get them out. Half-collapsed buildings may topple further at any moment, aftershocks may cause more collapses, and hazardous substances, such as gas from broken pipes, may suddenly catch fire. Extreme care must be taken during rescue operations in order not to put the rescuers at risk too.

Dragon's head

Bronze ball

SENSING VIBRATIONS
The first instrument for recording earthquakes was built by a Chinese scientist, Chang Heng, in AD 132. This seismoscope was a bronze vessel surrounded by dragons and toads, with a heavy pendulum hanging inside. Depending on the source of a particular tremor, one of the dragons would open its jaws, releasing a bronze ball into the mouth of a waiting toad.

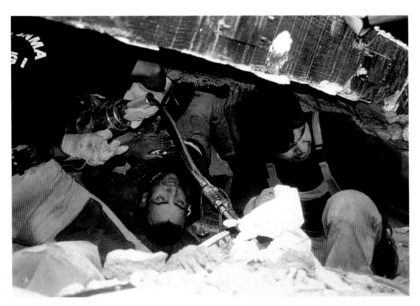

TRAPPED
The best way to free trapped people is to move down through the rubble alongside them. Attempting to clear debris directly on top of earthquake victims may loosen unstable rubble that could fall on them, endangering them further.

LISTENING OUT
A trapped-person detector can pinpoint the source of vibrations and sounds beneath a collapsed building using seismic and acoustic sensors. The sensitive device can distinguish between background noise and human movement and can even recognize the sound of a heartbeat.

Headphones to listen for human sounds

FEELING THE HEAT
A thermal-imaging camera uses infra-red radiation to detect the body heat of a trapped person through smoke and dust. The best time to use the camera is in the cool early morning, because at other times it can be hard to distinguish body heat from the natural heat of ordinary objects.

EARTHQUAKE SURVIVAL KIT
Because it is difficult to predict the exact time and place an earthquake will occur, many people living within an earthquake zone keep a survival kit in their home or car in case they are trapped or left without supplies.

Kit includes first-aid supplies, food, drinking water, and a torch

The Transamerica Pyramid has a flexible frame to cope with earthquakes

STRENGTHENED STRUCTURES
In earthquake zones, bridges and buildings are constructed with special features to reduce the impact of earthquakes. The foundations of the Transamerica Pyramid in San Francisco, USA, rest on a steel and concrete block designed to move with earth tremors, and the building's flexible frame allows it to absorb earthquake vibrations.

RESCUE PROBLEMS
Disruptions to electricity, gas, and water supplies, and to telephone and radio links, make rescue operations even harder. The devastation of the 1995 earthquake at Kobe, Japan, was made far worse by the failure of the water supply, which meant that firefighters could not put out fires. Further problems were caused by cars blocking the streets as people tried to escape, so that rescue teams could not get through.

Volcanic eruptions

AN ERUPTING VOLCANO fires molten lava, dust, ash, and hot gases up to 30 km (19 miles) into the air through an opening in the Earth's crust. Timely warning and evacuation are the best ways to save lives when a volcano erupts. Most devastating eruptions are preceded by days or months of smaller ones, giving plenty of time for evacuation. However, sometimes these mini-eruptions subside or an eruption may come without warning, making it hard to be precise about the timing. If a volcano takes some time to erupt after an evacuation, people begin to return to their homes even though the danger has not definitely passed. Some active volcanoes erupt regularly, while others only erupt every few hundred or thousand years. Volcanoes that were exhausted long ago are called extinct, but scientists have learned that even "extinct" volcanoes are capable of nasty surprises.

Umbrella protects evacuees from falling ash

FORECASTING ERUPTIONS
Seismographs, like these in the Vesuvius Observatory in Italy, are used to predict an eruption's timing and strength by measuring earth tremors, which often increase dramatically before an eruption. Striking changes in the shape of volcanoes may appear on satellite photographs just before an eruption, as the mountainside bulges from the force of the magma (molten rock) within it and the sea falls back from the shoreline.

DIVERTING LAVA
Red-hot, molten lava at temperatures of up to 1,200°C (2,200°F) can burn, bury, or flatten anything in its path. In some populated areas, aeroplanes bomb lava flows to try to divert their course. Elsewhere, huge dams have been built to protect cities at risk from possible mud or lava flows caused by volcanic eruptions. Lava flows are common in places such as Iceland and Hawaii.

EVACUATION
With sufficient warning, people can be evacuated from the area surrounding a volcano before an eruption occurs. These villagers in the Philippines have waited until the last moment, fleeing only as giant ash clouds form above the Mayon volcano to join thousands of others already in government evacuation centres.

Eruption of Mount St Helens, USA, 1980

Lava flow from Mount Etna, Italy, 1983

SMOTHERING CLOUD

In addition to molten lava, a vast cloud of ash, steam, and poisonous gas, called a pyroclastic flow, erupts from a volcano. The volcanic ash covers the surrounding countryside and can suffocate people and animals. The steam makes the cloud scorching hot, while the gas includes carbon dioxide and sulphur dioxide, which can choke living things to death.

VOLCANO WATCHING

Volcanologists monitor active volcanoes to try to predict eruptions. They measure changes in the temperature of lava and gas samples and in the size and shape of features of the surrounding land. When working near the intense heat of the volcano, a volcanologist wears a reflective silver suit.

GAS MASK

In addition to protective clothing, volcanologists wear gas masks when working near lava. This not only protects them from the harmful acidic gases given off by the volcano but also keeps out volcanic dust.

Filter

CHECKING EARTH MOVEMENTS

Studying the ground level with monitoring equipment can help volcanologists to detect tiny changes that may foretell an eruption. They also use tape measures to check cracks in the ground, which may narrow or widen from day to day.

Folding, portable tripod

Environmental disasters

INDUSTRIES THAT HANDLE flammable, toxic, or polluting substances, such as gas, oil, chemicals, and radioactive materials, have strict safety regulations. This is because an accident involving such substances can have a devastating effect on the surrounding environment. People, animals, plants, soil, and even the air can be affected, and the resulting problems can last for years. Radioactivity from nuclear accidents may remain for centuries. When such a disaster occurs, the first priority is to rescue injured people and evacuate those in danger. Rescue workers need special protective clothing and equipment to ensure that they do not risk their own lives. Then the situation must be brought under control, to stop the spread of pollutants, before the clean-up operation can begin.

OIL SLICK
When the oil tanker *Exxon Valdez* ran aground off Alaska in 1989, polluting 2,000 km (1,250 miles) of shoreline, 11,000 people helped in the clean-up. To remove oil, floating barriers can be dragged around the slick to stop it spreading, then it can be sucked onto another ship. On land, the sticky oil can be blasted away with high-pressure hoses.

NUCLEAR DISASTER
In 1986, a reactor in the Chernobyl nuclear power plant, now in the Ukraine, caught fire, destroying the building around it and contaminating the surrounding area. People nearby were evacuated, and a thick concrete shell was built around the reactor. Ten years later, workers rebuilding the road to the plant still had to wear protective face masks.

CHEMICAL LEAKS
In 1984, when poisonous isocynate gas leaked from the Union Carbide battery factory in Bhopal, India, over 2,000 people died from the choking fumes. Aid workers rushed to the region's hospitals to help treat the 500,000 people suffering from chemical burns, damaged eyesight, and breathing problems.

Chemical burns

To extinguish an oil fire, the flames
must be brought under control,
then the pipes must be closed to
stop the flow of oil and gas. The
slightest spark can re-ignite the
blaze. During the Gulf War of 1991,
Iraqi soldiers withdrawing from
Kuwait set fire to more than
700 oil wells. Virtually all the
world's 1,200 oil-firefighters
were rushed in to tackle the fires,
pumping in mud to stop the flow
of gas and oil, or using explosives
to "blow out" the flames.

BURNING OIL
Oil-firefighters have one of the most
dangerous jobs there is. The US firefighter
Red Adair achieved international fame
in his long career, attending many of
the world's worst oil fires, such as the
flaming Piper Alpha oil platform in
the North Sea, which caught fire in
1988, claiming 167 lives.

Animal emergency

IT IS NOT JUST PEOPLE who need rescue services. Animals can also be victims of environmental or natural disasters, accidents, or mistreatment. All over the world, rescue services such as the British RSPCA or the American Humane Association are devoted to rescuing animals. Some of these organizations take care of animals that surround us every day, such as pets and farm animals, and only deal with wildlife when wild creatures come into contact with people, for example when someone finds a baby bird that has fallen out of its nest. Conservation groups work with animals in the wild or on nature reserves. Some rescue workers, such as rangers on a wildlife reserve or veterinary staff, are trained and paid for their jobs, but many others are volunteers, devoted to their cause by their love of animals.

BEACHED WHALES
Scientists cannot explain why whales like this one sometimes lose their way and become stranded on beaches. Rescue teams often simply wait for the tide to come in, then ease the whale back into the water. In other cases, whales may have to be lifted into the sea in a canvas cradle attached to a crane, or even carried in trucks overland to reach a suitable deep water bay.

Garden netting

RESCUE SERVICES
Many countries have special animal emergency services that can be called in to rescue animals from hazardous situations, such as this tawny owl trapped in garden netting. These services also deal with mistreatment of or injury to animals, work to educate people on animal care, and provide free or low-cost veterinary treatment.

ENVIRONMENTAL DESTRUCTION
Animals that manage to escape from a natural disaster such as a fire or flood may return to their homes in the aftermath to find their habitat and food sources have disappeared. In 1998, many tortoises in the Galapagos Islands had to be evacuated by conservationists when their natural habitat was destroyed by the lava flow from an erupting volcano.

EXTINCTION

Throughout the world, the numbers of wild animals have fallen drastically as people have taken their natural habitats for farming, housing, or industry. Some species have become extinct, and others are threatened with extinction. To save endangered species, rangers monitor the animals' movements using devices such as the radio collar being fitted to this sedated elephant in Kenya.

Radio collar

RELOCATION

When a predator such as a tiger or a wolf wanders into an area close to humans or livestock and begins to hunt, local people often want to kill the animal in order to safeguard themselves and their property. Conservationists are called in to trap the animal and take it to a new location in a more remote place to protect not only the wild animal but also the people and their livestock.

Cleaning the feathers of an oiled sea bird

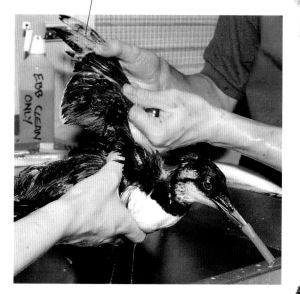

OILED BIRDS

Birds covered with oil from a coastal slick cannot fly or keep themselves warm, and may be poisoned simply by trying to clean themselves. Rescue workers carefully clean their feathers with special chemicals before returning the birds to the wild. Other animals, such as fish and marine mammals, are also harmed by such pollution, and its effects may last for many months.

Rescues from remote places

BEING LOST OR INJURED far from help in a forest, mountain, desert, or polar region can be a terrifying experience. Survivors of plane crashes, shipwrecked sailors, or lost explorers may be prey to such dangers as wild animals and a lack of food, water, or shelter, as well as extreme weather conditions. Alerting the emergency services can be a problem, although if radio contact is possible, stranded people can send an SOS message to rescuers. Survivors who cannot make radio contact must create clear emergency signals for any planes or ships that pass. With luck, someone left behind will alert the emergency services when a lost person does not appear when or where expected. Then a search can begin in the most likely areas.

British RAF Nimrod reconnaissance plane

SEARCH AND RESCUE PLANES
Military reconnaissance planes are used in civilian search and rescue missions over remote regions. They can survey vast areas of land and sea. Sensitive equipment on board detects boats and aeroplanes from long distances and in all kinds of weather. The planes may drop emergency kits to survivors, then the crew radios the location to rescue vehicles such as helicopters or lifeboats.

FOREST RESCUE
In a dense forest, people in need of rescue should search for a clearing that is open to the sky, so that airborne rescuers can spot them easily. Victims of plane crashes should remain near the debris, which will be obvious to people flying overhead. Creating a smoky fire with damp vegetation, cutting down a group of trees, or turning on vehicle lights should also attract the attention of rescuers.

EXPOSURE
When someone's body is exposed to wind, rain, or cold, it loses more heat than it can generate. Hypothermia victims must be moved to shelter and wrapped in blankets, such as this heat-reflective one, to slowly restore body temperature.

Foil blanket

SNOW RESCUE VEHICLE
To rescue casualties in remote, snow-covered terrain, emergency services can dispatch a paramedic on a snowmobile hauling a rescue sledge. The paramedic slides the casualty in at the back of the sledge and protects him or her with a waterproof cover. It can be a bumpy ride over snow, so the paramedic drives slowly on the way to the nearest hospital.

Casualty is transported on a covered sledge

E 5725

Polaris

M·4 VOL. MEDICA

SNOW EMERG

The survivors standing beside the snow-covered wreckage of their plane

SURVIVING AGAINST ALL ODDS

A plane carrying 40 passengers and five crew crashed on a snow-covered mountain in the Andes in Chile in 1972. At first, the 16 survivors ate dried fruit and sweets that they had brought with them and made soup out of lichens. When the food ran out, they started to eat the bodies of the dead passengers in order to stay alive. At last, after 71 days, the survivors were rescued by helicopter.

US Air Force LC130 plane equipped with skis for landing on snow

POLAR REGIONS

In 1999, a US doctor named Jerri Nielsen developed symptoms of cancer while working at an Antarctic research station and needed urgent treatment. The rescue crew had to wait for a break in the hostile weather before going to collect her. In order to ensure that the plane's landing gear did not seize up, it was vital that the temperature rose above −50°C (−58°F). The ski-equipped plane landed on a runway carved from ice, picked up Nielsen, and flew off without ever cutting its engines.

Staying alive

WHEN STRANDED in an isolated spot by a plane crash or a vehicle breakdown, the survivors' most urgent needs are food, water, shelter, and fire. The importance of these varies according to the location, water being the most crucial in the desert, and shelter the most vital in polar regions. Food supplies must be rationed because survivors do not know how long they will have to last before help arrives, and finding wild foods can be difficult. Attracting the attention of rescuers is the next task. Crash victims should stay close to the wreckage, as the debris should be visible to rescuers from the air. In addition, survivors can create signs that can be seen from above. Any signal that would not normally occur in nature should attract attention, such as a group of small fires or a large pattern made by scraping away topsoil to reveal the rock beneath.

SURVIVAL RATIONS
This small pack of survival food was carried by a British soldier during World War II. The high-energy, vitamin-enriched sweets and water purification tablets it contains were intended as emergency rations to sustain a soldier until he was able to find another source of food and water.

Compass

Heliograph (signalling device)

MILITARY SURVIVAL JACKET
In case they crash or need to abandon their aircraft, many military pilots wear special survival jackets to help them in a hostile or isolated environment. Stored in pockets and pouches in the jacket is everything needed for survival, from tools and weapons to a first-aid kit, a survival blanket, and signal flares.

Blanket

Knife with sharpening stone

Heliograph

Revolver holster

COMPASS
Survivors armed with a compass and a map should be able to work out their location and head for the nearest inhabited place. Even without a map, a compass can be used to ensure that the party keeps walking in the same direction, or to keep track of any changes in direction.

SIGNALLING
If a plane or boat comes into view, survivors can use a piece of polished metal or a specially made heliograph (signalling device) to create flashes of sunlight to attract attention. In this way, they can send a Morse code signal, such as SOS (Save Our Souls), a well-known international distress call.

SURVIVAL EQUIPMENT
A knife is an important asset in a survival situation, for building shelters, killing animals, and hacking through undergrowth. Soldiers and adventurers travelling in remote places always carry a survival kit including a knife, matches, a torch, signal flares, and a sleeping bag.

Survival knife used by British military personnel

FIRE

Lighting a fire is one of the first tasks that survivors should tackle. This will not only provide warmth and light, but also keep away animals and send a signal to rescuers. First the survivors need to find dry wood that will light easily, then they should clear away dry vegetation from the site that would otherwise catch fire. If weather conditions are very windy, the survivors can light the fire in a trench to shelter it and to prevent the flames from being blown out.

Making a shelter on a branch frame

TEMPORARY SHELTER

Long exposure to wind, rain, sun, or cold can be fatal, so finding or creating shelter is a top priority. A cave or rock crevice will provide instant cover, but if there is vegetation or debris available, it is not difficult to create a simple lean-to shelter. In a snowy environment, a hole facing away from the wind will provide some protection from the elements.

Directional-strobe cover

Tourniquet

F Need food and water

I Serious injury / need a doctor

Battery

Battery-powered emergency strobe

LEAVING SIGNS

If forced to move from the site of their vehicle's wreckage, survivors should leave signs to show their direction for potential rescuers to follow. In addition, internationally recognized ground markers (above) can be made big enough to be seen from the air, using sticks or stones, or by scraping away a layer of earth to leave clear markings.

Improvised stretcher

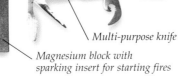

Ground-marker panels

Razor

Multi-purpose knife

Magnesium block with sparking insert for starting fires

FIRST AID

When people find themselves stranded in an isolated place, first-aid treatment must be given to sick or injured people as soon as possible. To carry an injured person, an improvised stretcher can be made with two jackets fixed between poles.

Space rescue

IF AN EMERGENCY HAPPENS in space, there are no rescue services nearby to rush to the assistance of the astronauts. The crew must deal with the situation themselves or by following instructions from Mission Control on Earth. The crew cannot simply abandon a damaged spacecraft or space station, because they will not be able to survive for long alone in space. The only solutions are to try to direct the damaged spacecraft back to Earth or to move to a rescue vehicle if one is available. Every accident or problem that is encountered and solved in space travel provides a valuable lesson for those in charge. For example, space shuttles are now fitted with an emergency escape hatch that enables the crew to leave the craft wearing a parachute during certain types of emergency.

Westar VI satellite

NASA RESCUE TEAM
If a space shuttle has to make an emergency landing, a special rescue team is ready on standby. The most dangerous situations occur if the craft comes down on land rather than at sea. Wearing special suits and masks to protect them from toxic fumes, members of the fire crew have the hazardous job of entering the damaged shuttle to pull the astronauts to safety.

Rescuer checks an astronaut during a practice drill

Solar panels for generating electricity

Soyuz spacecraft for transporting crew

Docking port for visiting craft

Crew lives here

Model of the Russian Mir space station

NEAR DISASTER
In 1997, a supply craft slammed into the side of the Mir space station, damaging the power source and causing an oxygen leak. The crew tried to launch the Soyuz spacecraft, which acts as the space station's "lifeboat", but, without power, the release system failed. Just in time, the sun caught one of the undamaged solar panels and restored the power, allowing the crew to set to work sealing the oxygen capsule and repairing the space station.

OUTSIDE THE SPACECRAFT

When an orbiting satellite is in need of repair, astronauts must leave the relative safety of their spacecraft to carry out essential work in space. For tasks outside the craft, astronauts wear a special type of suit, called a Manned Manoeuvring Unit (MMU). Once in this "flying armchair", astronauts can move around easily but have no lifeline to guide them safely back inside the craft. If they get into trouble, they rely on the rest of the crew to help them out of danger. Here the US astronaut Dale Gardner is shown making the first ever satellite rescue in 1984.

"Houston, we've had a problem."

APOLLO 13 CREW TO MISSION CONTROL, 13 APRIL 1970

APOLLO 13 MISSION

In April 1970, Apollo 13 was headed for the Moon, when 320,000 km (200,000 miles) from Earth, an oxygen tank exploded in the service module, and oxygen and electricity levels fell rapidly. The only way to save the crew was to use the lunar module as a kind of lifeboat to return to Earth.

Apollo 13 blasts away from the launch pad

Astronaut wearing a Manned Manoeuvring Unit (MMU)

Crewless craft for delivering essential supplies

The command module returns to Earth

PROBLEMS ON BOARD

Apollo 13's lunar module had sufficient oxygen and power to reach Earth, but was slowly filling with the carbon dioxide that the crew breathed out. Using items that could be found on board, such as plastic bags, cardboard, and tape, the ground team made a piece of equipment to clean the air. Following detailed instructions, the crew then built the same equipment on board.

HOME AT LAST

The crew huddled inside the lunar module, where the temperature had fallen to 3°C (37°F), the walls were covered with condensation, and the windows had frosted up. As the craft approached Earth, the astronauts put on their space suits and crawled back into the command module. They then discarded the lunar module and splashed down safely in the Pacific Ocean to everyone's great relief.

Into the future

WATER CANNON

This firefighting cannon shoots out jets of tiny water droplets at more than 400 km/h (250 mph). In this way it creates a large cooling surface that can extinguish huge blazes and even electrical fires. The cannon is fully portable and can be carried into the heart of a blaze on a firefighter's backpack.

SCIENTISTS ARE CONSTANTLY AT WORK on new technology that can make the difference between life and death in an emergency. The equipment used by rescue services is becoming more sophisticated, as well as smaller, lighter, and more portable. As innovations in materials make some equipment cheaper to manufacture and operate, it becomes more widely available.

Equipment for testing the boot

Rescue services are now faster and better equipped, and specialized vehicles rush the crew to the scene of an accident even in remote locations. Emergency medicine is steadily breaking new ground in the fight to save the lives of injured people, and safety mechanisms in vehicles and machinery are increasingly efficient. But even with all these advances in the technology of life-saving, the most vital part of any emergency operation remains the courage of the rescue workers who risk their own lives to save other people.

Boot with reinforced sole

TREADING CAREFULLY

These remarkable boots have been specially developed to protect the feet and legs of rescue workers as they clear land of unexploded mines. Tiny grains of resin-coated stone with air pockets between them make up the soles of the blast-resistant boots. The soles absorb the impact of an explosion rather than trying to deflect it like conventional blast-resistant material, and a tough layer next to the foot provides extra protection against dangerous fragments.

LIFE-SAVING SUIT

In an emergency, the wearer of this prototype arctic survival suit can use it to send out a distress call to attract potential rescuers. If the person becomes unconscious, the suit automatically sends out an SOS message. The suit constantly monitors the heart rate and temperature of its wearer and the surrounding weather conditions, and its in-built direction-finding unit allows it to pinpoint the wearer's exact location.

The emergency suit can aid survival in arctic conditions

A volunteer tests the suit's user interface

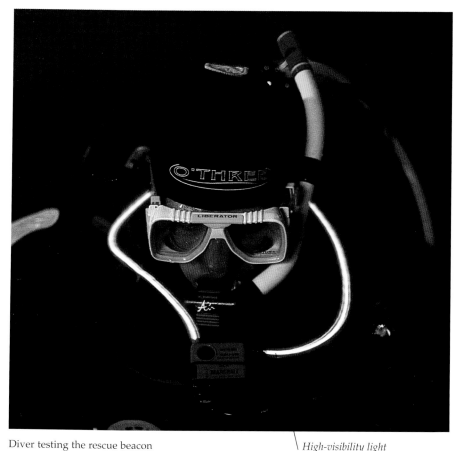

Diver testing the rescue beacon

High-visibility light

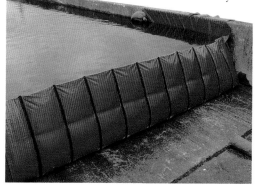

Emergency dam system

HOLDING BACK THE FLOOD
This triangular plastic flood barrier is designed to become rigid as it fills with water. The weight of the water makes a seal against the ground, stopping floodwater from leaking through. The dam packs flat for ease of transportation and can be re-used when necessary. It is far more effective than a traditional wall of heavy sandbags and can be constructed in a fraction of the time.

SAFE AT SEA
This battery-operated personal beacon device with a high-visibility flashing antenna can be worn by sailors around the neck and is particularly useful to people on solo voyages. The rescue beacon is set to the worldwide emergency distress homing frequency and can be activated manually by pressing a large button. If the device is immersed in water for more than 20 seconds, it automatically sends out a distress signal.

Flashlight is cheap and portable

Radar flashlight

SEEING THROUGH WALLS
Microwave beams from this flashlight can penetrate a solid wall, then reflect even the smallest movement caused by a person breathing, and show the results on a bar-graph display. In a hostage situation, the police will soon be able to use the device to monitor the breathing patterns of people on the other side of a wall and launch a rescue mission. The flashlight can detect movements up to 5 m (16 ft) away.

Exit sign used with directional sound evacuation beacon

HEARING THE WAY OUT
A new fire alarm system uses a directional sound signal to guide people quickly from a burning building, even in the presence of thick smoke. The signal is made up of pulses of noise comprising many different frequencies, to which people respond instinctively. As someone moves along the exit route, the signal at each exit beacon speeds up. When he or she approaches a flight of stairs, a rising pitch signal indicates the need to go up the stairs, and a falling pitch means go down.

Antenna and sensor

Mine-detector robot

Abdomen-like control surface

Artificial muscles move the robot's legs

Claw-like control surface

ROBOT LOBSTER
Ideas for rescue innovations come from many different sources. Scientists have been studying the movements of marine creatures to help them make more efficient underwater machines. Looking at the way in which lobsters move has helped them to create a robot that can operate on the seabed and in rivers by crawling along to search for mines.

Index

Acknowledgements

Dorling Kindersley would like to thank:
Kevin O'Sullivan of the London Ambulance Service; Juley Hickman of Sussex Police Uniformed Operations Air Support Unit, Shoreham-by-Sea; Steve Carpenter of the Ambulance Air Support Unit, Shoreham-by-Sea; Chris Witten, Sean McCaffrey, Andy Corke, and John Ralph of the Shoreham Airport Fire Service; Abigail Pritchard of UNICEF; Richard Eccles of St John Ambulance.
Design assistance: Sheila Collins
Index: Lynn Bresler
Additional picture research: Brenda Clynch, Lesley Grayson, Bridget Tily
DTP assistance: Nomazwe Madonko
The publisher would like to thank the following for their kind permission to reproduce their photographs:
a=above, b=below, c= centre; l=left, r=right, t=top
Aberdeen Fire Department, Maryland: 14b; 15t.
AIGIS Ltd: 62tr. **Alan Watson:** 56cl. **The Art Archive:** Dagli Orti 35t. **Associated Press AP:**

Hobart Mercury 34tr; Jeff Zelevansky 12bl. **Bridgeman Art Library, London/New York:** Grace Darling Museum, Edinburgh, Scotland 10br. **Bureau INF R. P. photothèque:** 23tr. **City Fire Museum, New York:** 11b. **Cockermouth Mountain Rescue Team:** 36b. **Corbis UK Ltd:** 10-11, 13cl, 60-61; Bettmann 57t; David Turnley 41b; Galen Rowell 57b; Gary Trotter/Eye Ubiquitous 27b; George Hall 56tr; Graham Wheatley/The Military Picture Library 33tr; Hulton-Deutsch Collection 28c; Jeffery L. Rotman 28b; Lawrence Manning 6br; Liba Taylor 40tr; Neil Rabinowitz 30-31; Owen Franken 43bl; Peter Turnley 24cl; Reuters New Media Inc 46br; Tim Wright 67b. **E. S. A.:** 60b. **Mary Evans Picture Library:** 9b, 44tr. **First Army Headquarters, Selimiye Barracks:** 44cl. **Georgia Tech, Atlanta:** 63cr. **Ronald Grant Archive:** Twentieth Century Fox and Warner Brothers 9t. **Kate Howey, Elgan Loane of Kentree Ltd, Ireland:** 12tr, 13br. **Hulton Getty:** 12cl. **Hydroscience Ltd:** 63tr. **International Committee of the Red Cross:** 7tl. **International**

Federation of Red Cross and Red Crescent: 40bl. **IFEX Technologies:** 62tl. **Kobal Collection:** Warner Brothers 8-9t. **Lynton Gardiner:** 16l, 16-17, 17r. **Magnum:** Erich Hartmann 12r. **Marine Science Center, Northeastern University:** 63br. **Mike McMillan/Spotfireimages.com:** 47bl. **H. K. Melton:** 29bl. **Museum of London:** 11cra. **NASA:** 61br, 61b, 61r. **Oxford Scientific Films:** M. J. Coe 55tr. **PA Photos:** 15b, 18cl, 26br, 37tr, 41tl, 41tr, 50t, 52cl, 53cl, 54tr, 55cl; Kai Pfaffenbach 29cl; Reuters 42bl; Robert Pratta 16cr. **Quadrant Picture Library:** 39cl. **RAF Museum, Hendon:** 58tr. **Reima Smart Clothing:** Arto Liiti 62b. **Rex Features:** 17tl, 18cr, 30cr, 50br, 52bc; Masataka Ooe 18b; Agence D.P.P.I 31cr; C. Harris/Times 33bl; D. Bagby 18tr; Fema/Sipa Press 19; Jacques Durieux 51bl; NASA 13cr; O. Globo 38tl; SIPA Press 46bl, 48cl; Uhuru 39t. **RNLI:** 6tr, Richard Leeney 32tl, 33cr; Alex Wilson 10crb. **RSPCA:** 54bl; Andrew Forsyth 43br. **Science Photo Library:** David Weintraub 50-51; Maximilian Stock Ltd 25tl; Peter Menzel 52-53; Vanessa Vick 52cr; W. Bacon 36tr. **Science Museum:** 25b, 44br, 48tr. **Sea Marshall Rescue Systems Ltd:** 63tl. **Seattle Fire Department:** Richard Leeney 33br.

Sound Alert Technology plc: 63bl. **Topham Picturepoint:** Associated Press 48-49b; Tim Ockenden 38-39. **TRH Pictures:** 45tl; 45br. **US Department of Defense:** Douglas J. Gillert 60cl. **Volunteer Medical Service Corps, Lansdale, Pennsylvania:** 22tr. **Weatherstock/Warren Faidley:** 46tr, 46c, 47tl. **John Wiseman, School of Survival, Hereford:** 58br.

Jacket credits:
Associated Press AP: back cover tl. **Cockermouth Mountain Rescue Team:** back cover cl. **Ronald Grant Archive:** back cover tl; Twentieth Century Fox and Warner Brothers front cover tl. **Rex Features:** Gill Allen front cover bc; SIPA Press front cover cb. **Royal National Lifeboat Institute:** Alex Wilson spine; Richard Leeney inside flap bc; back cover tr, front cover tl. **Seattle Fire Department:** back cover cr. **Topham Picturepoint:** Associated Press front cover cla.

Every effort has been made to trace the copyright holders of photographs, and we apologize for any unavoidable omissions.